On Comn
Grol

G000149497

A Programme for Teaching Poetry

Jill Pirrie

To My Mother and Father

"The world is troubled
With a lack of looking."

George Tardios

© WWF UK (World Wide Fund For Nature), 1994

Published by WWF UK (World Wide Fund For Nature),
Panda House, Weyside Park, Godalming, Surrey GU7 1XR, UK.

ISBN: 185850 000 1
Designed by: Anne Davison
Typeset by: Tradespools Ltd, Frome
Illustrations by: Anne Davison
Printed by: Arrowhead Printing Limited, Bordon.

WWF UK is a Registered Charity.

Contents

page

1 Introduction   1
2 Process   15
3 Ways of Looking   29
4 What is the Truth?   41
5 Writing for Christmas   53
6 A Wizard of Earthsea   75
7 The Poem and the Story   89
8 Water   101
9 Thresholds   119
10 Dreams and Hauntings   133
11 Poetry and the Environment   147
12 The Common Ground   163
13 Outlets   169
References   171
Acknowledgments   172

1 Introduction

The six years since the publication of the first edition of *On Common Ground* has been a time of unparalleled change as teachers have adjusted and adapted to the requirements of the National Curriculum. Course books have proliferated and many have been reductive, even trivial. Most, in the name of breadth and balance, have attempted to encompass the range of National Curriculum requirements through a huge variety of strategies. This new edition of *On Common Ground* will also address a range of new obligations. Most especially, it will assert poetry as a priority if these obligations are to be addressed within a programme which is neither reductive nor banal. The popular culture of our day in its advertising hoardings, television jingles and soap operas cannot be dismissed out of hand because it is an important part of our children's worlds. It is, however, only as children are empowered with the 'word' as it comes to them through the richness of their own and others' literary heritage that they are armed against the exploitation which demoralises as surely as it demeans.

Balance is not so much a matter of dividing a syllabus into equal components, as a matter of identifying the enabling idiom which gives access to all the various genres. Poetry is not just yet another means by which human-beings communicate. As the most structured and conscious form of language, it provides a sure route to literacy. Following the implementation of the National Curriculum, the aim of this new edition is breadth through focus. The focus identifies poetry as the unifying idiom which empowers children to reflect on the uses and pleasures of their infinitely adaptable language even as they develop increasing mastery.

Knowledge about language has emerged as an important issue within the National Curriculum and, again, poetry can be the impetus for work on history of language, dialect, grammar, and so much more. Poetry offers no soft option. The Chapter, "A Wizard of Earthsea", for instance, shows that only as children accept the constraints of the wizard/creative artist rôle can they be released to engage with their own and others' heritage and find their own voice. Only then is that heritage restored and renewed by and within each succeeding generation.

Language through literature is a rigorous route to literacy; it is also a sure one. As children learn their inherited grammar, they must learn that while its rules are not arbitrary, neither are they absolute. The features of our language shift and change as they adapt to the circumstances and requirements of new generations. This is a measure of our tribal power as we listen, speak and write. We must not exercise that power lightly,

1

but responsibly and sensitively, within the accepted, received forms and symbols of our literature. The music of those forms, caught in the rhythms and cadences of poetry, is both compelling and seductive. Above all, as teachers, we must not compromise children's literacy either by offering them an easy panacea of mindless grammatical exercises, or by retreating from our pedagogical role to the fringes of our classrooms and encouraging an equally easy conviviality which precludes reflection and rigour.

It was as a teacher of language that I found myself being drawn inexorably and inevitably into 'green' issues. That great parable of language, *A Wizard of Earthsea*, for instance, is also a parable of environment. The wizards must learn that power is inseparable from responsibility and that only as they learn to 'name' can they exercise that power. Similarly Ted Hughes's fable *What is the Truth?* is a surer insight into the need for care and respect for the creatures of this planet than all the didactic treatises. Environmental awareness cannot be taught in the English classroom; it can be inculcated at the deepest level through the special agencies of poetry, story, myth and fable. This book attempts to demonstrate some of the strategies which have encouraged the country children of Halesworth into a new awareness of their world. There is, for instance, the 'green' fable in the chapter "Writing for Christmas". It seemed entirely appropriate to link one of our great Christian festivals with a celebration of the seasons. As we reaffirm our dependence upon earth, we celebrate in a deeply religious sense; it is certainly as incumbent on Christianity to celebrate the riches of earth as it ever was on our pagan ancestors. Moreover, as children learn to look with the eyes of the poet, they learn to look as though for the first time ever. And this is the beginning of the environmental awareness which illuminates so many of the exercises in this book.

It is the central premiss of my work that personal experience is the basis of good imaginative writing. Very young children turn towards the world in a spirit of discovery and their lives are full of all the excitement, joy and tragedy which is the stock in trade of the writer. In the following extract, for instance, Carmel comes in from the playground to grapple with great issues of birth, life and death. Only through the special agency of language is her encounter with the snails shaped and structured. Most importantly, it is her words which transform the experience into a matter of importance.

I Saw the Fat Snail

I saw the fat snail and the fin snail a long time ago in the scool playground. One was crawling on to a leef and she was very annoyed becus the leef kept curling over and she was reely cross. How do I know, becus she kept prodding the leef wiv her horns but she didunt prod her frend. I dont know how her shell got broken. Mabe she had a fit while I was in scool. Some of the boys pushed her under the wire under a leef but she didnt stay and she came out agen. Why. I suppos her frend was loneley and had no one to play with. Next time I came I coodnt find her and looked under the broken house. You are going to get a surprise. Guess. No it wasnt a ladybird hiding. No it wasnt a marble. No not a little flower. No it wasnt a marble will you give up. Well there were tree baby snails. I havent decided on their names yet. Everybody says they dont wany horrid snails called after them. I think snails are quite pretty dont you. Where was the fat snail, you will never guess. She had climed up the wall into a little hole under a little blue flower and was dead. What did she die from. But she was so happy about her three babies wasnt she.

Carmel Maresa O'Mahony, 6 years

Not only are young children endowed with clarity of vision, they are capable of reflection. In the following short poem, for instance, surely Robert demonstrates a self-awareness gradually and introspectively developing into self-knowledge!

I have lotse of moods

I have lotse of moods
wen I am in a bad
mood I un'rolle the toilet rolle
when I am in a good
mood I rolle up the toilet rolle

Robert Shiress Whitson, 6 years

It is, however, eight year old Nika Turbina's anthology *First Draft* which most powerfully challenges and raises expectations. Yevgeny Yevtushenko says in his introduction: "This book makes one think that children perceive the world in a much more adult way than we think."

So often we patronise children with our easy assumption that they cannot apprehend the abstract. Maybe their lack of experience causes them to confuse the concrete with the abstract, and then, pleased by their amusing *naïveté*, we smile and make all those demeaning concessions. Children have a profound capacity for abstract thought and when this is linked with clarity of vision, poems like "Stop for an Instant" are written.

Stop for an Instant

Why,
when the time comes,
do we chase childhood out of the door?
Why do we try
to skip over the steps of days?
We hurry to grow up.
And we run
past all the years,
as if in a dream.
Stop for an instant!

Look,
we forgot to pick up
from the ground
dreams of red sails,
of fairy tales,
waiting for us in the dark.
I will run down the steps,
as if they were days,
to my lost years.
I will pick up childhood in my arms
and return my life to it.

Nika Turbina, 8 years

We should not simply dismiss Nika's anthology as the amazing product of a precocious talent, but accept it as representative of the latent talent within most children. Indeed, Yevgeny Yevtushenko says that while: "There is much that is purely private, diary-like, in this book . . . other children must have the same acute contemporaneity . . . and the aching sense of anxiety for our planet."

Then there are Nika's own words as she talks to the great poet: "When I write I have the feeling that a person can do anything if he only wants to."

Perhaps not "anything", but certainly children can achieve much that is remarkable. This is the burning optimism which must amount to a faith and inform the teaching in our classrooms. But then she continues: "There are so many words inside that you get lost."

And then we know that as teachers we must at least attempt to redeem the lost words if we are to release the gift in all our children. This is the way that they will find themselves. Perhaps then Yevtushenko need not say:

"Nika's poetic diary . . . becomes the diary of other children, those who do not write poetry." Other children need their own diaries. When they all write poetry, like Nika, they will know that whether they become poets in adult life is not important, "The important thing is truth."

While it is easy to accept that children must write from personal, first-hand experience, it is not easy to resolve the classroom problems this poses. These problems become more acute as children grow older. Upper juniors, lower secondary children crave excitement. Their own worlds seem pale and humdrum beside the worlds which they feel capable of creating. Their instinct is to reject their own world and to 'make up' stories and poems which, unhappily, are so often no more than banal, unconvincing flights of fancy. Paradoxically, the teacher must set boundaries, impose constraints, in order to set free. When we ask children to imagine, we are, above all, asking them to remember with a special intensity. Only then do we establish an authentic starting point for their writing. And so, two clear problems emerge:

4

1 How do we transform the limited, 'ordinary' experience of the child so that he turns to it as a source of interest and excitement, willing to relive it in a state of total involvement?

2 How, having achieved this involvement, do we help the child to a position of detachment from which he can apply his craft as conscious artist, subject to the rigour of his discipline?

I have found that these problems can be resolved only through a literature-based syllabus. There must be excitement. When we read, excitement comes through a vital moment of connection with the text. This is a moment when we recognise something we have noticed ourselves but never before truly realised, something which has been brought to our attention by the seeing eye of the writer. At one of these moments of recognition or identification comes a sense of surprised discovery. Suddenly our own experience attains new value. It is exciting, worth taking seriously. There is an episode in Barry Hines' Kes which unfailingly provides a class with a literary experience of this kind. The scene is a classroom in a run down urban school. The children are disadvantaged, inarticulate. One boy, Anderson, called upon to address the class, stands miserably silent. He can think of nothing worth talking about. The teacher urges "just something you've remembered."

Memory stirs. But Anderson is embarrassed. His own experience is too limited, too trivial to put into words. Shamefaced, he replies:

"There's summat. It's nowt though."

The teacher's reply is crucial:

"It must be if you remember it."

And so Anderson is released. No longer inarticulate, he tells his sensuous, exciting story of two small boys filling their wellies with taddies. One of those boys, Anderson himself, puts on the tadpole filled wellies. Taddies squash between his toes, spurt up his legs, and, of course, our own children cannot fail to make the connection. Like the class in the novel, they are "up to the knees in tadpoles".

Most importantly, through a literary experience, their own ordinary lives have been heightened. For a moment, they turn to the trivia of their own world with a sense of discovery; they make a first tentative step on the journey to self-acceptance. In the classroom, these fleeting moments cannot be harnessed at will, but we can be sure that our children's writing will testify to their reality. The prose account and poems which follow, for example, were written by children whose "nowt" had suddenly become "summat".

Memories

I remember . . . the taste of a dead moth that was hidden at the bottom of the linen basket for six months, all dry and soft like an old digestive biscuit. And eating too many Sinotabs and being sick all over Bruin the bear, and although I hadn't eaten carrot for three days it came out in neat cubes of red stuff. And I remember having banana split for tea, and throwing it at the cat, who rolled over in it and started to wash itself sitting in a pool of ice-cream with rafts of banana floating on it.

Once I was in my cot and I tried to climb over the side but it was unlatched and I flew under the cot. The carpet smelt like old socks and gone-off flour. In the corner there was a cemetery for flies, but worst of all near the leg, was a dead bird. I leaned forward and touched it, but it fell apart leaving a labyrinth of maggot holes like an old statue, riddled with woodworm. I remember following a sprayed fly, walking as if it had just drunk a bottle of whisky . . . and pulling the legs off a daddy-long-legs.

Memories are like books because you can look back time and time again on Memories you never knew you had.

Thomas Croft, 12 years

Gem

She looks hopefully at us.
She longs to feel the breeze touch her nose.
At the jingle of her leash,
She leaps ecstatically.
She yanks at her leash outside the gate.
She pleads to go to the marsh.
Again.
She senses things I cannot smell or see;
The smallest insect on a blade of grass,
The smell of a caterpillar's trail on a leaf.
She cocks her ear to sounds
I cannot hear:
The sniffing of a vole,
The wind passing through birds' wings.
I wonder what she is looking for.
She shies away from other dogs.
She is black and white and getting old . . .
We found her in the snow.

Oliver Cooper, 12 years

The Journey

The train pulled away,
Another rhythm on the rails returning
The early morning sunlight
As fresh as a new fall of snow
Pure and untouched.
A splinter of sunlight glinted on the window.
Fields wrinkled away from the line,

One looking like velvet,
Tractor marks – brushing it the wrong way.
A deer – playing tag with my eye,
All its limbs
On loose hinges
Ran into the trees.
Startled
Rabbits dotted about,
Mistaken for tufts of rotted grass.
Then . . . the odd disused station
Holding many a memory,
Waiting for a new coat of paint
And like an old clock
Waiting to be wound up.
The train shuffled through the countryside
Like a caterpillar

Until . . .
Slowly, it slurred to a stop.
My journey's end.
I opened the door
And stepped out
Onto a platform
Buzzing and busy.

Heidi Masters, 12 years

Fossil

Small detail sustained in time, right down to a fish's scales,
Printed shadow and light.
A shell protecting its treasure,
never to be broken.
A stone skeleton.
A snail a thousand ages old,
Bailed out into the cold rock . . .
Hard prints of a once lived life,
Light filtering the mind's eye
Until the world's shape is moulded into stone.
Corrugated iron, rock, cobweb?
Ridged-ribbed-rock.
Grooves engraved into mud, into rock, into our minds.
Or a wax-moulded chrysalis, waved, wax burnt to a crisp.
I touch it. It is taut,

Pulled into naked design
And left to be folded and kneaded into shape
In the soft rock –
Made into hard rock.
God's art work is in the form of a fossil.

Jessica Brown, 12 years

The Tree Climb

The plum tree, rough and rotten,
Crumbles under my numb hands.
The branches are old
And as I climb, they shudder beneath me,
The blossom streaming off in angry chains, pink and fluffy.
Close up, I see the grooves and wrinkles in the trunk;
I smell the rough pattern of the red leaves
And can almost taste the rusty bark.
In the centre of the tree
I am in my own rainbow world,
Cut off from traffic, people, noise,
Everything.
Everything, except the blossom and the smell of the scarlet bark.
I climb down and the tree is still
And almost scary.
The garden is deserted – beneath the fluffing branches,
And the falling blossom.

Matthew Shepherd, 10 years

Chicken Lucky

I walk into the yard,
Mud squelching into my sodden boots.
The hen, a Sussex Black,
Struts, casting her foot into healthy mud.

The chicks tail behind her
Their tinsel-like down
Blows as a baby's ruffled hair.

I move suddenly, tugging at my boot;
The chicks scatter, all but one.
I step on a soft lump,
Like a sponge.
I lift my boot, and it reveals . . .

Dark red pipes and tubes
Moving as the chick lies,
Mouth wide, gasping for breath,
Eyes half closed,
Legs kicking widely into space,
Clawing for a hold.

Until . . . like a wound-down clock,
They stop,
The eyes closed
Like an old man's.
They're grey and wrinkled.
I murmur a prayer
As other chicks use it
To clamber over.
The sticky grey tinsel
No longer fluffy.

I go for a shovel.

Caroline English, 13 years

★★★★★

The Thought-Fox

I imagine this midnight moment's forest:
Something else is alive
Beside the clock's loneliness
And this blank page where my fingers move,

Through the window I see no star:
Something more near
Though deeper within darkness
Is entering the loneliness:

Cold, delicately as the dark snow,
A fox's nose touches twig, leaf;
Two eyes serve a movement, that now
And again now, and now, and now

Sets neat prints into the snow
Between trees, and warily a lame
Shadow lags by stump and in hollow
Of a body that is bold to come

Across clearings, an eye,
A widening deepening greenness,
Brilliantly, concentratedly,
Coming about its own business

Till, with a sudden sharp hot stink of fox
It enters the dark hole of the head.
The window is starless still; the clock ticks,
The page is printed.

Ted Hughes

Memory is, of course, only the first stage (albeit a crucial one) in the imaginative process. The child poet remembers first, then selects and patterns. It is in these subsequent stages, the moment of conscious expression, that he detaches himself from his experience. Herein lies another intriguing paradox: these young poets must be childlike, artless, and yet, at the same time, artful. It is the teacher's dilemma to resolve this paradox. Again, my own solution lies within literature: in this case Ted Hughes's poem "Thought-Fox", followed by a reading of the poet's own explanation of the poetic process in *Poetry in the Making*. In his explanation, Ted Hughes shares with the children the way in which "The Thought-Fox" came to be written. He lets them into a secret (and secrets are always exciting!). As fellow writers, they listen and begin to grasp this underlying paradox of the poet's task, between the intensity of his involvement in his subject and the detachment he needs to subject this material to the poetic process. Within the resolution of this paradox lies the tension from which poetry is made. Hughes's statement:

"It is a fox and a spirit. It is a real fox."

shows us that a fox in a poem is at once a particular fox, and one which contains something of all foxes everywhere. The children's attempts to write their own "Thought-Creature" poems must also be based upon close and accurate observation of one particular creature. But they must also aspire towards universality: they must represent spirit as well as substance. I have found twelve to thirteen year olds quite capable of appreciating the complexity of their task and yet excited, rather than daunted by it. The less able grasp it at an intuitive level and often, surprisingly, write with a particular strength and clarity.

The Thought Cat

There was a bowl
Of cream in the kitchen.
Inside my head a cat mewed
And spelt its name 'Cat'
In creamy letters.

The cream was a projector screen
Which enabled me to see the cat.
He was licking his paws and cleaning his face,
Getting ready to JUMP,
JUMP out of my thoughts and into reality.
I looked at the bowl of cream.
There was my cat,
Drinking the cream,
My cat.
I reached out to stroke it.
It leapt out of my reach
And curled up by the fire,
Purred and melted away
Into my memory.
My cat for ever.

Marie Fenn, 13 years

The Thought Fish

The fish swims a circle . . .
Life without an end.
Always he looks outwards, out of his bowl.
Then he makes a sudden dash
For the bridge,
And charges out the other side
Like a torpedo,
Smashes through his bowl and floats
Into my mind . . .

Where he still swims in circles,
A wandering thought.
His tail waves like an old Japanese fan,
Pushing him forwards.
His scales glimmer –
The very first solar panels.
All the while he feeds,
Sucking up all the old memories . . . and . . .
All the while he grows . . .

He grows and grows,
Until, too big,
He bursts through my mind,
And into my pen . . .

And out onto the paper
Where he forms words,
Which in turn, turn into a poem.
A poem about a fish.

Matthew King, 12 years

And so the children begin to realise that the raw material of poetry exists trapped within their minds. In so far as all children have memories, all children are embryo poets.

John Gordon, one of our leading writers for children, says in his essay in *The Thorny Paradise*, "On Firm Ground",

"The starting point must be a place which already exists, we cannot free ourselves from what we know, and Mars is still landscaped on earth. A rigidity is necessary; imagination must be anchored . . . "

As teachers we must accept and teach the terms of this rigidity. Only then can we set children free to achieve some small part of their potential.

2 Process

Much of the teacher's task lies in guiding children through the process of writing, while at the same time preserving the freshness and spontaneity which must be the hallmark of their work. I have found the following exercises teach structure and, at the same time, respect the integrity of the writer's ideas.

To begin with, a reading of Jacques Prévert's 'To Paint the Portrait of a Bird'. The work which follows has something in common with Sandy Brownjohn's 'The Making of . . . ' exercise described in *What Rhymes With Secret?* In many ways the painting of a picture is like the writing of a poem and a reading of 'To Paint the Portrait of a Bird' directs attention to the way in which we handle words. Clearly, the Noun/Name is the strongest part of speech. The children see that, as poets, they are, above all, Namers. They learn that each individual has his own identity contained within his uniquely magical first name. Power lies in that first name. As poets we must search rigorously for the right Name or the spell won't work. Secondly, they come to see the Verb as second in importance only to the Noun. Again its effectiveness lies in the precision of its use. As the poet's tool, it must be fine, resilient, appropriate to its task. Similarly, what better way to learn familiarity with these common grammatical terms than within a context of reading and writing poetry. At the same time the children learn the strength of the active, the comparative weakness of the passive. They practise making conscious, delicate decisions. They discover how complex is the poet's task when he tries to write most simply and clearly. This exercise can come as a necessary corrective to the intelligent, 'literary' child whose writing all too easily becomes loose with ill-chosen or redundant adjectives or adverbs. Children must learn to write with economy and discrimination, and to guard jealously the power of their nouns. They must also discover that there are no rules which cannot sometimes be broken to good effect. Always I stress that poetry is written to be spoken, that sound and meaning must harmonise. They must develop an ear sensitive to the music of their words.

Jacques Prévert's poem also teaches something of the seriousness of the artist-poet's work, the depth of his commitment as he waits for the idea:

> 'Sometimes the bird comes quickly
> but he can just as well spend long years
> before deciding
> Don't get discouraged
> wait
> wait years if necessary.'

And . . .

> 'When the bird comes
> if he comes
> observe the most profound silence.'

Ideas, like birds, are elusive and I believe a deep, relaxed silence is necessary if children are to write poetry. The classroom is normally an unsatisfactory environment for writers. The close proximity of so many bodies means endless distraction, but these children at least deserve silence.

Then there is the insistence that we judge our work by the highest standards:

> 'If the bird doesn't sing
> it's a bad sign
> a sign that the painting is bad
> but if he sings it's a good sign
> a sign that you can sign . . .'

And so the children write their own 'To Paint a . . .' poems. Again they try to balance an intense memory of their subject with the conscious detachment which chooses only the best materials and wields the truest tools. They do not copy or parody. Rather, Jacques Prévert has provided them with a framework for their own perceptions and observations. Through receiving his voice, they find their own. I hope that this is at its best the 'creative mimesis' which Peter Abbs argues for so strongly in *English Within the Arts*. At times the children's writing is clear, strong and simple. When it is, they have reconciled the subjective and objective aspects of their craft.

To Paint the Portrait of a Bird
To Elsa Henriquez

> First paint a cage
> with an open door
> then paint
> something pretty
> something simple
> something beautiful
> something useful . . .
> for the bird
> then place the canvas against a tree
> in a garden
> in a wood
> or in a forest
> hide behind the tree
> without speaking
> without moving . . .
> Sometimes the bird comes quickly
> but he can just as well spend long years

before deciding
Don't get discouraged
wait
wait years if necessary
the swiftness or slowness of the coming
of the bird having no rapport
with the success of the picture
When the bird comes
if he comes
observe the most profound silence
wait till the bird enters the cage
and when he has entered
gently close the door with a brush
then
paint out all the bars one by one
taking care not to touch any of the feathers of the bird
Then paint the portrait of the tree
choosing the most beautiful of its branches
for the bird
paint also the green foliage and the wind's freshness
the dust of the sun
and the noise of the insects in the summer heat
and then wait for the bird to decide to sing
If the bird doesn't sing
it's a bad sign
a sign that the painting is bad
but if he sings it's a good sign
a sign that you can sign
So then so very gently you pull out
one of the feathers of the bird
and you write your name in the corner of the picture.

Jacques Prévert
(Trans. Lawrence Ferlinghetti)

Transformation

I watch as a ship sails serenely by.
And using my mind as a pencil,
My eyes as paints,
I sketch a warship from the waves.
And my pencil
Turns the blue-grey sea

Into blue-grey steel.
As a stupendous wave whirls up,
A transformation is made
From wave to ship's chimney,
From foam to smoke,
Vanishing into space.
My eyes turn to land,
The barren, brown land.
It distorts into another warship,
Not modern now, wooden.
From Hermes to Mary Rose.
As a lifeguard's flag comes into sight,
She has a pinnace now – and life.

Alison Enticknap, 12 years

I include the following poem written as a result of the Sandy Brownjohn exercise 'The Making Of . . . '; firstly, because it has much in common with the foregoing poems, and secondly, because it demonstrates a delightful sense of fun. Poetry writing of all kinds demands complete commitment; this does not preclude enjoyment. The two are interdependent.

The Making of a Hornet

For the body,
Take a piece from dad's best rugby shirt,
Shrink it,
In a wash that is far too hot,
Dry it,
In mother's new tumble-dryer,
Crimp it
In your oldest sister's crimper.

For the wing,
Make up the recipe for glass.
Bake
In hot oven till soft;
Roll out with gran's best rolling pin;
Cut
In two and stick firmly to body.

For the legs
Untangle eight of the hairs from grandad's beard.
Intertwine
Two together so you have four pairs.

For the brain
Unhook Aunt Maeve's best duffle coat.
Cut out
The British Home Stores ticket inside.
Feed it with knowledge for five days,
Then let it breathe in a dark cupboard.

For the buzz
Take the first sound your telly makes
When you switch it on.
Then nourish it on other buzzes.
Next,
Embroider this buzz into the brain.

Then roll up into a ball,
Flutter his wings
And let him call.

Rachel Harrison, 12 years

Following this exercise comes a reading of extracts from writers' notebooks. Access to writers' notebooks gives the children a sense of privilege. They feel initiated into the secrets of the writer's mind and again there is that essential ingredient of excitement. Gerard Manley Hopkins' detailed observations of water, the way it behaves, the manner in which a wave breaks, are read alongside artist Leonardo da Vinci's detailed recordings of trees, water, creatures reproduced in *Penguin English Stage One: I Took My Mind a Walk*. The details of the observations are impressive. The fact that writers may keep notebooks in much the same way that artists may keep sketchpads has wide implications for the children. Most especially they begin to appreciate the need for constant re-drafting.

Aug. 13 – Heavy seas: we walked along the sea wall to the Kennaway Tunnel to watch them. The wave breaks in this order – the crest of the barrel 'doubling' (that a boatman said, is the word in use) is broken into a bush of foam, which, if you search it, is a lace and tangle of jumping sprays; then breaking down these grow to a sort of shaggy quilt tumbling up the beach; thirdly this unfolds into a sheet of clear foam and running forward it leaves and laps the wave which reaches its greatest height upon the shore and at the same time its greatest clearness and simplicity; after that raking on the shingle and so on, it is forked and torn and, as it commonly has a pitch or lurch to one side besides its backdraught, these rents widen; they spread and mix and the water clears and escapes to the sea transparent and keeping in the end nothing of its white except in long dribble-bubble strings which trace its set and flow.

From the Journal of Gerard Manley Hopkins

And so the children attempt a simple prose account of a process they have observed or attempted themselves. It may be a craftsman at work, the way in which a fire burns, anything which requires of them a detailed analysis of the process and then a careful drafting and redrafting until a piece of clear, accurate prose emerges:

Unblocking a Drain in Winter

The wave started to gurgle above the drain gate. The day was cold and the water had a thin layer of ice on the top of it. I took a good hold of the glove. It was frozen solid. I held the glove tight and smashed it on a wall, over and over. A shower of jagged ice fragments fell to the ground and broke into a thousand pieces of glittering beads.

The glove was big and had about half an inch spare on each finger. The water inside the glove froze on my hand like setting jelly. I walked over to the drain and bent over and clamped my fingers under the grate. It reminded me of a spider's web. The coldness soon penetrated the rubber glove and I hadn't even put my hands in the water. Cramp soon set in so I had to stop. I sat down with my hands in the air watching my fingers straighten out until they could not move. I sat in a certain amount of pain waiting for my fingers to right themselves.

For the second time I tried to unblock the drain. I put my hand in the water. I reached down to find the bottom but the water started to seep over the top of the glove. It ran down the inside and started to fill up each of the fingers. As the water rose in each finger the cramp began. I stood up and flung the glove, water spraying on the ground and started huffing and puffing on my hands to keep them warm. Bother the glove! I just stuck my hand in and cleared it. I felt the bottom and scooped a handful of mud and leaves out. My hand was like a mechanical digger. I brought out five loads of mess. A job well done.

Ian Self, 12 years

Christopher Nolan's account of the plucking and gutting of the Christmas turkey in *Under the Eye of the Clock* also serves as an evocative and compelling model. A simple study of the verbs as the resilient tools and the nouns as the materials of this craftsman/ writer equips children to write their own account of a process. Their account must, at least, aspire to the same accuracy, economy and clarity.

Wielding a sharp knife Nora cut off the lonesome, guilty looking head, then she cut off the scaled-skin legs. Next she slit the turkey open and forced the flesh to yield. She eased her hand up into the cavern. A huge gllomp sighed from the depths within. She began to pull. The expression on her face matched the sounds from the dead. At last she pulled the innards outwards. Another resurrecting plurpp issued with the issue. She left her booty upon the newspapers. With blood upon her hands she eased her fingers down inside the throat skin and pulled until the windpipe broke. She held the ringed cord in her fingers for a moment as if measuring its length. Back down the trembling throat curled her fingers again. "I'm trying to catch the crop," she explained, her voice throaty with trembling. He could see her fingers bothering the breast skin. Then they ripped out the crop. It looked like a burst balloon and was inclined to twist around her fingers. Turning her attention then to the offal saturating the newspapers, she separated the liver and the blueshot purple-edged gizzard from the sluggish green guts. Parcelling the bilious remnants, she went outside to place them in the waste bin. Returning to her bloody task she picked up the heart. It had clotted blood nestling in its chambers. She dropped it into a bowl of water. Then she showed her children the gall bladder, which was attached to the liver. She explained about its green contents, and cutting away the green sac, she placed the liver in the bowl. Now she slit open the turkey's stomach. The gizzard was full of grit, corn and shale. Nora removed the contents and washed the gizzard, then she brought it back and showed the watching pair the golden wrinkled lining within the stomach muscle. Finally she carried the dismembered corpse over to the sink, asked Yvonne to fetch the drum of salt and purifying the bird she left it to drain on the stainless steel sink.

From *Under the Eye of the Clock* by Christopher Nolan

Gutting a Goose

One misty night my dad goes off with his gun under his arm. He is off to a marsh called the Banana Marsh as it is in the shape of a banana. He hides in the bushes and keeps very quiet until he hears a goose flutter up into the sky. He lifts his gun to his shoulder and takes his aim and fires; he hits the bird in the head and it falls to the ground. THUD! He trundles back to his van along the muddy path. When he gets back he heaves the bird into the back. When he reaches home he says,
"Here you are, Mother," and hands the bird to my mum.
She replies by saying, "Oh, brilliant."
Next morning the bird is completely forgotten about until I walk into the kitchen and see it lying there on the work-top. It stares at me with its big beady eyes. Mum comes down having forgotten about it as well and just wanders into the kitchen and she nearly jumps out of her skin. Later that day mum gets out her bin-bag and starts to take off the feathers. I usually help but I decide to sit and watch instead. The more she plucks, the room fills with more feathers. She tries to put them in the bag but they just fly out again. It looks like a snow scene from the middle of winter. I am asked to pick them up but I just sit and watch them float to the floor.

Dad comes along with his big knife as soon as mum has finished plucking off the down (which is used in pillows and duvets). He usually has to ask where about to cut as he never remembers.

First the feet are cut off, then the wing tips, then the head but he leaves some of the neck to make the gravy. A slit is cut across the bottom. There is usually a thick layer of yellow fat which is round the body as well. When he finds the insides, he starts with the green intestines which he pulls for yards and yards. After this he finds the crop. This is a pinky colour and is very hard. It grinds up the goose's food. The stomach, heart, liver, kidney all come out as one lump. GLOOP! on to the newspaper. We need to save the heart, liver and the part of the neck to make the gravy. Once we've made sure that the bird is cleaned out in the insides we wash it thoroughly before putting it on a tray.

I am usually allright when I watch this. My brother backs off each time it is done. I am usually the one who is made to put the newspaper in the bin. The worst is it stinks of rotten fish. The smell lingers around the house for days after this task is done.

Just think what my dad has gone through just for our Sunday lunch.

Tracy Martin, 12 years

Naming through the Senses

The 1960s made central the child and his experience, particularly the way we all explore the world through our senses. There is no doubt that this preoccupation led to certain excesses. Sometimes the pouring out of sensuous detail was unselective and unstructured. Nevertheless there was excitement in the genuine attempt to enable children to write honestly. Today we must remember that the senses are not only the means by which we explore the world and know that we are alive; they are also the means by which we remember. Past events are recalled by a fleeting, evocative smell, an associated sound; we see with our 'mind's eye' when we recall. Hence, when we ask children to imagine, the sharpness of their perceptions derives directly from sense impressions. While the 1960s emphasised sensuous experience, previous decades required that great writers be absorbed and imitated. Today, I suggest, the way forward lies in a synthesis of these attitudes. By reading a wide range of fiction and poetry, children absorb the symbols of our culture; by listening to the cadences and rhythms of others, they learn structure and find their own voice. The following exercise took place within a context of reading and speaking a wide range of poetry.

First – a matter of drafting, note making: remember a place you know well and write observations, each one relating to one of your five senses.

The Wood Shed

1 Hearing   a lawnmower cutting grass, a tractor rumbling, a blackbird chirping with all his might, a dog barking, the buzzing of the bees, someone getting out a saucepan, a rustling of a mouse.

2 Sight   a spider creeping across the floor, sunlight sifting through the gaps in the wall like little snowflakes.

3 Smell   a smell of newly cut grass, musty smell of soil and wood mingled together.

4 Touch   rough wood, crumbling soil, an old piece of carpet, wet soil, slimy slug, corrugated iron rippling, a sharp splinter.

Phoebe Wingate, 11 years

This is, of course, an artificial exercise. Our senses are interdependent and cannot be classified in this way. Nevertheless, it harnessed an act of intense memory to the necessary self-consciousness of the poet. Later the poem emerged from these notes through an act of deliberate craftsmanship:

Wood Shed

I'm hiding
In a very good place.
Someone's footsteps tap past.
In the distance, a tractor,
Maybe ploughing.
It's a faint distant rumble
Like far away thunder.

A musty smell tickles my nose,
And soil clings to an old spade
Like barnacles to a rock.
Someone's started a lawn mower.
Suddenly, a huge, hairy spider creeps out.
I look around me . . .
A flower pot.
I put it on the spider.
Shouts of "I've found you!"
And "Where's Sally?"
A blackbird chirps
With all his might.

Buzzing bees work at the flowers
And then a scramble of rough paws
Rushes to the end of the garden.
A dog starts to bark
And sunlight sifts through the wall
Like little snowflakes . . .
Quiet again.

Phoebe Wingate, 11 years

The following poems similarly show deliberate recall of sense impressions crafted into an art form:

Senses

Taste
The dry, musty leaves
Which tamper with the air.
Lingering smoke,
The taste of ash.

Hear
The clip of the shears
As they prune the hedge.
Listen to the leaves
As they throw a tantrum
In the wind.

Smell
The sweet fragrance
From soft brown apples
Feasted by wasps,
The dusty corn
Thrown from the yellow harvester.

See
The rust colour
Painted through the garden.
See the bee,
Flying,
Weighed down by boots of yellow pollen.

Touch
The leaves
Crumbling with dryness.
Feel the bitter night
In the air
Of my autumn garden.

Ruth Kingshott, 13 years

Farmyard Chatter

There they are, every day without fail.
Leather breath and graciously plodding,
The local gossips.
Listen to them whisper, listen as they trip
Over the caked ground.
Fresh straw . . . smelling like that
Box of Weetabix I opened last week,
Sizzling silage in large grey tanks.
Hear it bubble, then splurt against the cold tin.
Breathe in,
And your lungs will fill with roasting dung
And fresh cut grass.
I passed through that farm;
The smells pierced the back of my throat.
And those graciously plodding local gossips
Whispered and stared.

Emma Buckingham, 12 years

The Old Chicken

The old chicken cackled
Like an old woman,
Her beak strung open,
Gasping for air.
Her eyes,
Like deep holes in her head,
Sunken and dull.
She blinked, slowly, in the dim light.
Eyelids flicked down, and up again,
Thin flaps of skin,
Like scales of a snake.
Her crimson crest flopped over her left eye
Like a red beret.
The wattle, a double chin
Or a pink scarf,
Flapped as she turned her head.
Scaly legs,
Like the body of a worm,
Fold and wrinkle and loose flaps of skin.
Tail feathers overlapping one another
As a fan of cards.
The old chicken gargled softly
As if trying to sing herself to sleep.
Then pecked slowly in a puddle in front of her.
The barn was dark.
But a patch of light lit up the two hen boxes in which she lay.
Her neck hung out of the box
Like a dog's tongue from its mouth
And dangled limply in the puddle.
Her eyes closed, as if still sleeping.
She gargled no more.

Sally Clifton, 12 years

Flaming June

The pond skaters
Skate on a tightened elastic band
Stretched too far.
It breaks with a snap and a plop
As a gold fish moves.
Ringlets flow out,
Like the ripples in a wavy hair style.
The cress weed with coal roots
Grows through the wire bird-stopper.
My tadpoles, like two developed apostrophes,
Live in amongst that cress,
Legs of it making a slalom course
Upon a sloping ledge.
A frog sits sunbathing
On the waterlogged branches
Of a fallen tree
And the fiery sun
Suntans the field
Towards its future harvest.

Emma Graves, 13 years

Birth

Within the blood of the nettles
And the scorch of the sun
On a bed of plaited moss you will find it.
Surrounded in dandelion sweat and apple sap
And a grassy green stain upon its spine,
It lies there, a bundle of bones in one heap.
The earth around it has the smell of coffee beans,
Freshly ground coffee beans.
In the background you can hear
The chorus of the cars climbing the hill
And the thud, thud, thud of the child's ball upon the ground.
Around the tiny cluster of veins and bones,
Are a thousand green needles
Threading the rain from tree to tree
And weaving cobwebs of willow silk.
The continuous drip of the clay rusty drain pipe
Is the lullaby for the baby rabbit.

Emma Buckingham, 11 years

3 Ways of Looking

Our children must learn that if their poetry is to work it must surprise. More
must realise that it is the poet's especial task to reveal the surprising within the ordinary.
I have found the following exercise – 'The Magic Image' – a means of discovering the
bizarre, the surreal, where we least expect it; in the everyday. This everyday world, as
we receive it through our senses, is unstable, fluid and shifting. Constantly, we are the
victims of delusion. Our eyes are deceived by tricks of the light, shadows, reflections.
Eroded rocks become menacing faces; cracks in the ceiling move and pattern as we stare
at them.

We begin the exercise by reading 'Water Picture' by May Swenson. Here the illusion
of reflection makes 'magic images' in such a way that we find the extraordinary within
the familiar. As usual, we have all seen these images. But we have not realised them.
May Swenson, because she is a poet, awakens us to these facets of our past 'ordinary'
experiences. Again, this is a moment of identification with the text when that vital connection is made and our own experience realised and externalised. Further, when we
look at a reflection as though for the first time we cannot help but write in metaphor.
We simply accept the evidence of our eyes in a childlike poetic way. Usually when we
look at a reflection in a window our mind censors what we see so that we separate the
three layers – the glass, the reflection, the scene outside. It is when we resist this censor-
ship and look with the poet's eye that we enter a bizarre, surreal world in which

> 'The newsreader sits
> Talking in the garden;
> The cats tread on his face.'

Thorsten Merriott, 12 years

or in which

> 'My face is a pond.
> The outside fence surrounds
> My nose, a goldfish
> Breathing . . . '

Victoria Mawer, 12 years

Water Picture

In the pond in the park
all things are doubled:
Long buildings hang and
wriggle gently. Chimneys
are bent legs bouncing
on clouds below. A flag
wags like a fishhook
down there in the sky.

The arched stone bridge
is an eye, with underlid
in the water. In its lens
dip crinkled heads with hats
that don't fall off. Dogs go by,
barking on their backs.
A baby, taken to feed the
ducks, dangles upside-down,
a pink balloon for a buoy.

Treetops deploy a haze of
cherry bloom for roots,
where birds coast belly-up
in the glass bowl of a hill;
from its bottom a bunch
of peanut munching children
is suspended by their
sneakers, waveringly.

A swan, with twin necks
forming the figure three,
steers between two dimpled
towers doubled. Fondly
hissing, she kisses herself,
and all the scene is troubled:
water-windows splinter,
tree-limbs tangle, the bridge
folds like a fan.

May Swenson

Following this comes a reading of 'Images' by George Tardios. His opening words:
'The world is troubled
With a lack of looking.'

30

are the basis of discussion – if only we would look, we would find the magical within the commonplace. Again, we see that the world, as we receive it through our senses, is not stable but subject to change, illogicality. Sometimes our own response to the world connives with the illusion to make a deeper magic:

Images (Cyprus 1961)

The world is troubled
With a lack of looking.
I sing my songs.
The world sleeps.

I see the sky reflected in my teacup.
I move the cup
and I tilt the sky.
The flying crane is shadowed
On the mud wall.
My shadow touches his
And I ride the bird.

The stars are mirrored in a pool
Of rain.
With my hand I scoop up the water.
I have a handful of stars.

I grasp the branch of a tree.
The wind blows
And the tree shakes my hand.
The moon shimmers on my glass of cognac.
I drink
And taste the moon.

I climb a fig tree and look down.
The earth has fallen.

My mother's face appears
On the surface of an olive.
I split the olive
And scar my mother's face.

All the world
All the world pours in at my barred window.
I lower my lids
And dam the flood.

George Tardios

Many of the 'Images' poems written as a result of this exercise are a response to the comic: the serious made foolish, the upside-down, the inside-out, the back-to-front. There is, in most of the poems, a delightful recognition of the foolishness of human beings at the mercy of their sensuous experience. Children also discover that in a poem an image may be auditory, olfactory, or tactile, as well as visual. For instance, the subject 'Echoes' may well come within the scope of the 'Magic Image'.

I find that not only does this exercise produce worthwhile writing; it is also, and perhaps more importantly, a key point in the process by which the child learns to make connections, sometimes bizarre, in order to arrive at a greater truth.

Reflections

The rushes on the banks of the lake
Stretch out to touch.
The reflection of the old mansion
Is so still . . .
A painting,
A perfect mirror image.

A pond skater on a lily
Pulls on his boots,
Laces tight.
Off he goes.
He spins around and around,
Dancing on his reflection,
Stretching it.

A frog jumps.
The water pot spills,
The painting runs.

Gemma White, 12 years

Reflections

Ripples on a pond
Delicate and mild,
Yet ferocious,
Dividing your head
In a bloodless way.
The water settles,
Like tracing paper
The surface traces the sky;

It films the moving,
It reads you
Like a book,
Uncannily,
Upside down, and backwards.
This time,
The dog does not jump for the bone
Yet tries to stroke the underwater cats
Who dart, like their cousins,
For a safe haven.

The pond is liquid quartz.
A two-way mirror
For the water beetle.
A transparent cover‾
Better than steel
For it can never be dented
By the swift blow.
A water beetle
Does not know what he is,
For the water can cause him no
Reflection
Which he can like or loathe
To have inflicted
Upon himself
Night or day
To haunt him,
Taunt him;
Or is his mind too small
To worry?

Clifford Black, 13 years

Reflection

I sat and stared
At a world I knew,
But didn't.
The reflection rippled
On the oily surface
Of the vase.
The light was pink,
My face dark.
The table hung

Like a hammock,
And the walls
Domed in around me.
The fruit bowl was swollen.
Over the side of the vase
Drooped wilting flowers
With petals like waxed pencil sharpenings.
And as I reached to touch one,
My hand, green, grew
And fingers stretched and widened.
My little finger
As big as the rest,
And my hand looked unbalanced.
I held the room;
From one end of the table to the other
Loomed my fingers.
As I let go they shrank.
And I just sat and stared
At a world I knew.

Thea Smiley, 13 years

House of Reflections

I see my face in the saxophone,
Stretched and curved.
Sun slides round it
And bounces off the walls.
The zig-zag pattern of the carpet
Sinks into the shiny black piano,
And I move in the dead television.
I see my two selves in the photo glass,
Years between us.
Sun on the garden bird bath makes wavy
Sea patterns on the ceiling.
Leaf shadows sweep across the wall.
Everything moves and all is still.

Oliver Cooper, 12 years

Reflections of War

The innocence of a summer garden
Projected onto the glazed window
Filters through, from the outside.
The newsreader's comical beard
Of bush and bramble
Lightens the shadow of brutal war
Where the bang of mortars
Sends a flock of birds fleeing
And a shell flings itself headlong
Into the oncoming sparrow,
Showering the shrubs in shrapnel.
A great and lumbering tank
Rolls over the horizon,
Crushing delicate rose petals
Under monstrous tracks.
Camouflaged troops hide in hedgerows
Where rabbits scatter before
Truckloads of refugees
Who must escape the farmer and his gun.
Then, the curtains are drawn,
And we return to the bitterness of war.

Timothy Leicester, 12 years

The Well of Deep Reflection

A single image
Drives frogs into twins
And height accounts for depth . . .
And dank density,
Light to light.
I see myself at the bottom . . .
Or the top?
Light is imperfect, but ripples
And the silky texture of green moss
Does but darken the stony wall.
The water laps and licks,
The water laps and licks back . . .

To cast images of infinity
With stony white clouds splattered
Like raw meringue.
Birds have doubled into wind witches
Strewn over Southern Russia.
A fortified hollow cylinder
With rippling glass inbetween.
Dark crevices hide weary toads
And streamlined newts
With doubled heads and doubled tails.
The water splashes and bubbles,
The water splashes and bubbles back.

I reach for a stone,
And he does too.
I drop it to the watery sky.
As it falls to its friend,
They hit the water and spatter.
Shrapnel flies.
And I reflect no more.

The water splinters and spatters,
But there is no reply . . .

Alec Thomas, 12 years

Moon Thoughts

White
Against the dusky dome of sky,
Painted with stars that spin white light wetly.
Old,
Marked black from soot and ashes
From its own long ago funeral,
Its sunken in face imprinted
On its crusty dry surface.
Channels thrashed in by once flowing rivers,
Icy and bubbling like a frosted breeze,
Choking with weed and bright eyed fishes,
Roots and trees bursting from the ground,
Like green silk thread pushed through cloth
On a flashing needle.
People laughing, buying round, bright fruit
From market stalls with stout ladies,
Mountains sprayed with snow like shaving foam
Peeking, piercing the dark blue sky,
Like swords buried in the ground.
Then . . .
The river's icy channel, filled with emptiness,
Only fishes' bones imprinted on dry rock.
Rock on rock, rock on rock.
The mountain's pinnacle is grey and dry.
The lake's hole is dry and splashed with dark.
The people are gone, the bones melting into
The vast whiteness, crumbled with charcoal.
There is no form of life,
But many forms of death.
Shadowed by the darkness around it,
It spins on, its surface rolled with black ink.
The face on its face does not smile.

Emma Walkey, 12 years

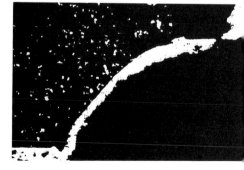

Seen Through the Lens

Again, the theme is the 'Magic Image', and the purpose is to make the child conscious of his looking and aware of the immense difficulty of his task, while at the same time, releasing the urge to write. When we use a lens, we look with a deliberation, an intensity. There is a moment of transformation and there are various facets to the experience: the three stages by which the transformation occurs. For example, if the lenses belong to binoculars, the stages are:

1. The scene through the naked eye – hazy, indistinct.
2. The act of focusing. The moment of transformation when the sense of sight becomes curiously independent of the other senses. We can now see in close up but we cannot hear, smell, taste or touch. So we are in the scene but not of it. We are detached observers.
3. The binoculars are removed – the scene hazy, indistinct as at first. This poem may have a circular shape.

A poem to initiate thinking is 'In the Microscope' by Miroslav Holub. I find also that good colour photographs of cell structures under a microscope provoke interest and discussion.

Seen Through a Lens

The rock's grey outline jutted out
Like a filling in an erupting tooth
From a sea of green gum.
A climber hangs from a fishing line rope,
A red spider
Hanging from its thread
Contrasting brightly against
The dull coloured rock.
I lift my binoculars.
Everything has a rainbow edge.
Then,
I see the texture of the rocks
And the wrinkles in a climber's coat and trousers.
I feel the determination
In his expression.
It is as though I can feel the whistle
Of the wind
And the rustle of his anorak.
I put down my binoculars
And once again the rock juts out greyly
And the climber is
The spider, small and vulnerable,
Hanging from its thread.

Stephen Cook, 12 years

Seen Through the Lens

A motion of clothes,
A stick as thin as a single
Horse's hair.
He sits on a matchbox waiting, soundless.

A circle of perfection,
A magic, magnifying circle.
The sleeve of his jumper, dirty
Where he put his hand in the maggot box.

The pond has mini-waves,
Tench for whales,
Pike for shark.

His rod tip sways,
Sways silently.
His bream is a shark,
His dream is hopeful.

A motion of clothes,
A stick as thin as a single
Horse's hair.
He sits on a matchbox,
Hopeful.

Trevor Guyton, 12 years

4   What is the Truth?

I have found *What Is The Truth?* by Ted Hughes one of the most exciting and challenging books to be published for children in recent years. Subtitled 'A Farmyard Fable For The Young', it is an anthology of poetry with the poems linked by connecting prose passages continuing the theme of fable. This fable theme gives the poems an underlying meaning which persuades children into considering the nature of their own imaginative writing. Story is, of course, the proper vehicle for such abstractions. Children are able to apprehend the abstract at a very early age when it comes to them in this guise.

The book begins with God's Son being curious; he wants to find out about this earth and, in particular, mankind. He asks his Father to take him on a visit to earth;

'travel broadens the mind.'

God is doubtful:

'Mankind cannot teach you anything. Mankind thinks it knows everything. It knows everything but the Truth.'

The Son persists and, at last, God leads him to a village hillside and proceeds to summon the villagers to ask them questions in an attempt to arrive at the Truth. The farmer comes first. His task is deceptively simple:

'Tell us about one of the creatures on your farm.'

The farmer speaks poetry but finds the 'Truth' of the partridge strangely elusive. One by one the villagers speak poems about the creatures they know so well. Some come tantalisingly close to the 'Truth'. Always, however, the linking prose pieces keep in mind the futility of the poet's search. It is a fruitless search because it is endless. Words are clumsy, slippery. When patterned into metaphor they sometimes almost find Truth.

In this fable, however, God is consistently dissatisfied with the villagers' efforts. Here is the ultimate criterion by which poetry is judged. Sometimes He is pleased because there is so much surprise and delight in images coined so unusually and yet truthfully, of cows:

'And there's a ruined holy city
In a herd of lying down, and chewing cows.'

of farm horses:

'huge plum tight haunches revolving heavily
like mill wheels.'

of swallows:

'Blue splinters of queer metal . . .'

God's dissatisfaction with the poems as a whole is, of course, the supreme dissatisfaction of the poet – however he chooses and patterns his words, the permutations are endless, limited only by our human condition.

Paradoxically, however, the situation is not hopeless. If only we could put the right words in the right order, then we would arrive at the Truth. The *possibility* is always there. In a way these villagers are trying to emulate God's act of creation when He named these creatures and they came into being. The villagers' naming can be an approximation only. And yet again and again Ted Hughes makes us feel that it is indeed possible. We are even made to feel that, given the right words, the flesh and blood creature would appear before our very eyes; such would be the power of its Naming. Intellectually, however, we know such a power is beyond the greatest of poets. In fact, the nearer we come to the Truth, the more we realise our distance from it. And excitement builds. Throughout the book there is the tension of knowing that, in the end, the onus will be on God to answer His Son's question:

> 'But have we heard the Truth?' asked God's Son. He still had no idea what
> the Truth might be.
> 'No, not the Truth,' said God sadly. 'Not the Truth.'
> 'Then tell us the Truth,' said God's Son. 'What is the Truth?'
> 'The Truth,' said God finally, 'is this. The Truth is that *I* was those worms
> ... And the Truth is,' God went on, 'that *I* was that Fox. Just as *I* was that
> Foal ... I am each of these things. The Rat. The Fly. And each of these
> things is Me ... It is. That is the Truth.'

Unhappily, this is a Truth which we cannot comprehend. The Infinite is beyond our human experience and so we are unable to make the necessary connection. Just as in *Paradise Lost* Satan's accessibility engages our sympathy, while God remains remote and nebulous, so, here, ultimate truth is beyond our grasp. Our preference for Ted Hughes' animal poetry to God's stark

> 'I am each of these things.'

is however, an affirmation of our human condition rather than a rejection of the Infinite. Again, there is the essential paradox – the only genuine ending to 'What Is The Truth?' is an unsatisfying one. Perhaps most importantly, at the very end, God's Son stays here on Earth. Further, as the dawn rises, there is a doorway:

> 'And the middle of that cloud glowed like the gilded lintel of a doorway
> that had been rubbed bright.'

It is Man's destiny to aspire to the impossible. And this truth frees the children to make this aspiration their own. They are challenged into a deep commitment to search their memories, find the right words, work within the discipline of the poet's craft in an effort to answer the question *What Is The Truth?* for themselves.

I have found it works well to withhold the actual book from the children until after they have written their own poems. First, the fable can be explained, read to them and some of the poems read aloud. The classroom then becomes the hillside and each child, a villager summoned by God to speak poetry about a creature of the village. That essential ingredient of excitement lies not only in the challenge of the writing but in the eagerness with which, having written their poems, the children search through the book for Ted Hughes' attempt at the Truth of their chosen creature. With the audacity of the young, for a moment, they treat the great poet simply as a fellow writer, like them constrained by his human condition in his search for the Truth. Certainly, this exercise teaches that we succeed as poets only when we know we cannot ultimately do so. This is the paradox which must never be resolved because it provides the tension from which the poet's excitement derives. It is the essential flaw. When children discover it, they develop a deep commitment.

What Is The Truth? also helps the teacher in his attitude to assessment of the children's poems. Some teachers feel that they should not judge a child's poem. They feel they must, at all cost, accept. They feel, moreover, that as a child's poem is an honest attempt to say what he means; if it is criticised, it is debased. I believe that it is possible to respect the integrity of a poem and, at the same time, to criticise positively. The overriding aim, however, is that the children themselves should judge their own poems by the highest criteria. Through a book like *What Is The Truth?* they begin to learn for themselves the supreme dissatisfaction of the poet. Through the story they identify with the villagers and see that, beside ultimate Truth, their efforts are stumbling approximations. They have begun to absorb and understand the criteria they must apply to their own work if they are to write well.

The following poems, I feel, at least contain surprises which aspire towards that universality which comprises something of all tadpoles, cows, moles, bees, grasshoppers, cats everywhere. They are brave attempts at the Truth. It is no accident that all these poems have won national awards. Such is the magic of *What Is The Truth?* in an ordinary classroom.

The Tadpole Is . . .

> A priest,
> Swimming amongst his congregation,
> And wearing a rough robe of black
> As he preaches to the shimmering stickleback.
> The tadpole . . .
> So soft, but so swift, and speedy, and slick.
> The tadpole is an ink smudge
> Spilt from the finest of pens.
> It quavers like a shrill note,
> Then stiffens to that one pose.
> The tadpole is a stowaway.
> Hiding.
> Evacuating from its every home.
> No safe place to hide for the tadpole.

Michelle Barnes, 12 years

Cat

I saw it . . .
Suspended in a dull spectrum of
Straight edges curved
And muzzy sharpness.
Black from Shadow and Birth,
Light and Earth.
Caught with its hand in the till.
Found out.
A simpleton,
In a deep velvet gown,
Soft and cuddly . . .
No.
A hardened criminal,
Wearing a balaclava and jumpsuit.
Wads of ill-gotten notes
Lie bulging out everywhere
On its burnt wood body,
Cracked into a thousand tiny snippets of wire.
Its puffed out sleeves are
Crowbars, heavy with power,
Light with arrogance.
Bulging long at one end,
Short at the other,
Studded with diamonds of lead.
Its face held me,
As it held itself,
Clear, yet shrouded,
Showing itself naked
As a poor creature caught
In some harmless mischief.
But hiding the charlatan.
A black angel,
Hell-bent on hell.
Whiskers and nose,
Probing out a victim.
Eyes,
Gold watches streaked by fire,
Glazed, corrupted,
Yet totally in command.
Almost.
Ears,
Fat feathers pruned to perfection

Arranged tastefully in black fur.
Twin cloth caps
Rakishly placed,
For its old-fashioned interests.
And its tail,
Young and vibrant,
Boasting to do anything.
But the reality is nothing.
Its teeth,
White splinters from a cracked china marble.
The implements in ten hundred deadly games.

Scene : Anywhere.
Suspect : The Cat.

Accused.
Gone.

Stephen Gardam, 13 years

The Grasshopper

He's been wound up,
then set off,
springing like a mad flea.
His yellow body of patterned plasticine
springs in and out like a trampoline.
His slim grim face
and his cold slit eyes
seem to stare, but not see.
He's the grasshopper.
The wound up green jet.

Helen Ward, 11 years

The Cow

Warm desperate eyes
Looking down on me
Pitifully, as if it was terrible to be human.
Ears folded like wrinkled up shavings;
Softly smiling mouth with strings of spit
Hanging from the gentle pinkness of lips.
Warm smelly breath reaches out to

The cold air like the steam from boiling milk.
Wet nose like a sponge
With drips of mucus running down it,
Then mixing with the strings of spit.
The udder is baggy with milk,
Drooping down towards the cobbled ground.
Shoulders sticking out
With skin pulled tightly around them.
And the tail – muddy and soaked in rain
Swishes carefully from side to side.
The cobbled yard is embedded in
A layer of mixed-up cowpat,
Steam rising thickly from it.
The cow, a beautiful caring creature;
And we take her milk,
And sometimes her calf and her life.

Kirsty Butcher, 11 years

The Fly

The fly is a scurrying maid
humming a tuneless melody as she works,
cleaning the unseen traces of sweetness.
She cleans around an empty mug,
her legs moving like a nimble gymnast
walking the beam.

The maid is a fearless creature,
always entering without being invited,
not afraid to remove rotting food,
her translucent wings fixed to her body,
folded down to make a crocheted shawl.

The maid has lemon-fresh wits,
sharp, sour and bitter.
She walks on my bare arms,
her light legs gently tickling me.
I move my arm, command her to leave,
and she hurries away, only to return
through another door.

The maid spots a spider's web.
The dusty silk threads tempt her,
this web which looks like fishing line,
and has similar purpose:
but to trap a fly, not a thrashing fish.

The maid flies into the line,
and is caught;
her body struggles like a fish on land,
her furry legs splaying in different directions.
Angrily she hums, sounding like water
hissing on a stove.

The maid is exhausted, her shawl is split,
her charring overalls are hung up.
As the angry humming fades
I feel sorry for this maid,
always hurrying, scavenging for food.
Even as her busy life
leaves her.

Caroline English, 13 years

The Pheasant

The pheasant is the convict of the bracken world,
as he runs stumbling haphazardly.
A line of beaters stands ready to advance.
The signal is given
and the air rings
to men's bellowing voices
and sticks banging the bracken
that cracks under the frying sun!
The convict is sighted
and the only way is up,
up into the vast empty palette they call the sky.
He takes off like an unco-ordinated puppet,
but where is the get-away car?
As the pheasant heads over the trees,
the enemy works the puppet.
He looks down the silver-plated kaleidoscope eyes
at the double barrel gun
and in a feather ruffling
Screaming

eyes rolling second,
the pheasant falls like a clod of soil
earthed by a shot that drained the Electricity of life.
A last nerve flickers
and he dies.
Now he hangs by his neck in our garage.

Hannah Edwards, 12 years

The Goldfish . . .

is a splinter of mineral,
mined by Neptune.
Nothing stirs
in its own narrow world of undisturbed peace.

Its comfort . . .
reflection.
The duel begins –
a quick bolt from watching eyes
from above,
a challenge with no end.

The goldfish is a sort of . . .
delicate feather
made from tiny mirrors,
reflecting everything beautiful.
Its eyes look like frogspawn
with minute tadpoles in the middle.

I feed it. I clean it. And talk to it.
But I get nothing in return . . .
As if its body is here,
yet its mind is in a coma far, far away.
I wonder if it can hear me.
I get nothing in return
from this delicate splinter of a fish.

Adam Hughes, 12 years

Death of a Mole

A furry drawstring purse
Wobbles through the field.
Blind in the upper world
But a ruler downstairs.
Its body black
But its nose brown from furrowing,
All its tunnels dug out gently,
Not ploughed like a bulldozer.
The calm pace of its scuffing
Makes it a genteel ruler.
The mole is not a savage,
But dinner coils past,
The purse opens
And dinner rolls into the inner lining.
Hunger satisfied,
The mole scurries on up to our world,
Blind again.
The farmer has his shovel;
The guillotine descends.

Matthew Shepherd, 12 years

Stick Insect

A stick insect is a spy.
He watches your every move . . .
Dangling from a twig
Unseen, unheard.

Cunningly disguised,
The secret agent of the insect world
Blends into hazy surroundings . . .
Thin ridges on his body
Like bark on a privet bush.

He moves his wire legs
One by one
Slowly scaling the steep plastic walls
Of his sweet jar home.
He has feet like feathers
Never loosing their grip.
Antennae swivel, tuning in to the radio.

We never see him eat.
Maybe he is anorexic
And yet the twigs come out,
Peeled of their leaves.
I suppose he must binge!

The end of his life is nigh.
No one wants a retired spy.
His discarded skin lies
In the sand at the bottom of his home,
White and shrivelled,
A corpse of memories.

Marilyn Rust, 13 years

The Truth of a Bullfinch

Last night it happened . . .
There on the wood painted doorstep
the murderer had left it.
The light orange of its breast
clashed with the colour of the bricks.
It lay with its head slightly flattened
against the concrete.
Cold, dead, no reviving.
Its eyes, closed,
Slits like button holes
in a baby's waistcoat,
and rimmed with an outline of black.
Its feet were cushioned in its stomach.
Its loose plumage blowing
in the wind like sewn-in segments
of feathers from its tail,
divided into five
different colours.
Then, its black helmet, where underneath
its black eyes were hiding.
Its beak, the colour of slightly burnt wood,
thick and ugly.
And its black wings
brought closely together, rolled up
like the ends of two cream horns.
Next was its tail,
a spatula, slightly bent.

And there it was . . .
propped against the doorway,
unable to venture through the storms and the sunshine,
left in its death.

Hilary Foster, 13 years

The Bee

The bee is . . .
a seed,
never been planted,
caught in air currents,
forever,
until now.

The bee is planted into my brain,
already growing into my life.
Its body . . .
a pencil shaving
curled up
and held together by elastic bands.

The wings are wound up, then released
like aeroplanes won at the funfair
(sold by the man with a London accent),
but which break on their first flight.
Each wing is made from . . .
decomposed leaves
half turned into loam
so you can see through them.

Its dance,
unique,
speaks to you . . .
left, up, right, down.
Dr Dolittle's tango of the night
is finally translated.

Adam Hughes, 12 years

5 Writing for Christmas

In Vol. 3 Issue 1 of "Suffolk Education News" Fred Sedgwick writes:
"... can we have some work ... that accepts the reality of the Bethlehem event as it probably was? This means a bit of squalor, some cold, a feeling of being left out, and poor, of being a sort of refugee. Heaven knows there is plenty of scope in the world of today for the raw material such work needs ... Christmas should bring out the best. And schools look gross arranged like Selfridge shop windows with music arranged by Mantovani, and the poetry supplied by courtesy of Patience Strong."
Yes, the Christmas story is a tough story and must not be debased in our schools. But because it is a tough story it is a perfect subject for poetry, the toughest language of all. Such is the influence of our consumer society with its accompanying stereotypes and clichés, that it was many years before I dared trust children with the Christmas story as a subject for their writing. Of course, my apprehensions were ill-founded. Children are realists. They are able to slough off the glitter and tinsel and write with an impact and relevance which gives the old story a new universality. If this is to happen, however, there must be direction in the form of constraints imposed by the teacher. Only within those essential constraints will freedom of expression be realised.

A sense of purpose is also vital. In the case of the Christmas poetry which follows, the purpose lay within a sense of audience. This poetry was written for Halesworth's annual concerts of Christmas Words and Music. For many years I had prepared speakers. Children learned the Christmas poetry of Leonard Clark, Charles Causley, Ted Hughes and many others. They learned the pleasure to be found in entertaining others through performance, and, further, it was a means by which they learned by heart readily and willingly.

I was unwilling to believe that children could write their own Christmas poetry without lapsing into cliché. I was afraid to risk the freshness of their vision. As an adult, above all, I feared sentimentality. Children try to respond appropriately. Would these children of a consumer society produce 'appropriately' stereotyped images of robins in the snow, Bambis sliding on ice? On the other hand, there was the tantalising possibility that they just might express their own vital apprehensions of a story as old as time and as new as the present moment. They might succeed in telling the toughest story of all in the toughest language of all. Of course, as we saw in *What Is The Truth?* this kind of success is an impossible hope. But within the aspiration to succeed is the energy which will produce exciting poetry. I believe that the various themes which follow, at least, enabled these children to write with a freedom and freshness of expression which, at last, I had dared to hope for.

The Witnesses

Clive Sansom's poem "The Innkeeper's Wife" describes the stable in concrete, everyday images. Many years after the Birth, the innkeeper's widow takes a carpenter into the stable to do repairs and finds her memory stirred.

> "She rested on the straw, and on her arm
> A child was lying. None of your creased faced brats
> Squalling their lungs out. Just lying there
> As calm as a new-dropped calf."

Because the visitor is a carpenter, much of the imagery has to do with wood.

> "Too many memories lurk
> Like worms in this old wood. That piece you're holding –
> That patch of grain with the giant's thumbprint –
> I stared at it a full hour when he died:
> Its grooves are down my mind."

The language is immediate, the rhythm prose-like, catching the cadences of everyday speech. And these country children were able to make connections. Many muck out stables daily; some have their own horses. Reality began to impinge on tradition. But still a fresh direction was needed and out of this imperative grew the idea for a verse drama in which witnesses would come to the stable and speak the truth of what they saw. Because the Christmas story is timeless and universal, they would come from across the ages and each would speak within the constraints of his or her particular rôle. Their needs, preoccupations, interests, even prejudices, would give each a different and colourful perspective on the old story. First we discussed the Biblical rôles, people who might have been there that night 2,000 years ago: a carpenter, a traveller, maybe even a Roman soldier. Then came witnesses from across Time: an artist, a schoolboy, a poacher, a gipsy, an actor, all as compelled to speak of what they had seen as their Biblical counterparts. Last came a sleeping child. She came to the stable door in her dreams and as she looked for the first time ever, she too became part of the great heritage of story through which we try to make sense of the world and our own place in it.

After the poems were written, the selection made, I provided a linking narrative.

The Reunion

Narrator: One night, unknown ages after the first Christmas, a strange company met at the Inn in Bethlehem. Each was drawn by the memory of a winter's night when a young woman and her husband had found shelter in the stable. A baby had been born that night. And there had been witnesses. Now they must speak of what they had seen, share memories, search for the truth of what had really happened.

The Roman soldier was the first to speak. Trained to kill, ambitious for glory, then posted to a distant province, he had become bored and had strayed into the Inn in search of wine and good company. Then, he heard a baby cry.

The Roman Soldier

I looked and saw a light in a shed;
The pale yellow glow beamed through stone cracked walls.
My shield and sandals clattered over the cobbles.
I lay the sword against the wall
And the belt swung wildly,
Knocked over the silver sword
Which landed on soft dewed grass
Blessed by God.
I saw shepherds with crooks like pikes,
Angels with harps like bows.
But the woman smiled and looked down . . .
On a baby.
Not a baby who sang a song of war,
But one who smiled at me.
And though the fire looked like the fire of a siege,
Time stood still . . .
As I looked at the baby
And the baby looked at me,
As if it had seen the soldiers I had slain,
Knew the stories of my wars.
And my heart beat like war drums,
But he lay, forgiveness in his eyes.
I looked up and saw . . .
A dove high in the rafters,
With an olive leaf in his beak.

John Debenham, 13 years

Narrator: Then the carpenter rose and told of a night when he looked for a job and found a King.

The Carpenter

A soft glow through the broken stable door
Spread fingers of light into night air.
That door will need new woodwork soon,
I thought as I entered.
Then, my thoughts stilled . . .
People gathered around a manger.
And from the manger, a newly polished pine glow . . .
And a baby wrapped against the cruel chill.
A Boy Child who looked up at his mother
With secure, intelligent eyes.
The bond between mother and child
Was as tight and strong as any dovetail joint . . .
Nothing like the crude woodcraft of the manger.
The father stood at the mother's side.
The callouses on his hand mirrored those on mine.
And truth fell into place.
This was the one spoken of . . .
The Son of God.
I would follow Him . . .
With the strength of oak wood.

David Lewis, 12 years

Narrator: Next came a traveller. She told of a night when it was cold in the fields and the light from a stable welcomed her and gave her shelter.

The Traveller

The warm air, as sweet as milk,
but as sour as blood.
A woman lay on the hay;
To me, just another traveller.
The gentle drip of mucus,
as it ran down the cow's face
and fell on her sleeping calf
was like a rhythmical drumbeat.
I shifted in the brown hay
which stuck in my back,
but was comfortable enough.

Then, a smoky taste in my mouth
as a kitchen maid came in.
Her clothes and hair smelled of a bonfire
and made the air taste of ash.
Soon I was half asleep,
but half of me clung to reality . . .
the smell of rotting wood
floated through the air.
And, as I watched,
the patches of damp slowly spread across the walls.
And I heard a baby start to cry.

Sunta Templeton, 13 years

Narrator: Then, suddenly, there was a loud knocking at the door. Each guest remembered the night when he too had knocked at a door. There had been a welcome. And on this night too there must be room at the Inn for all who come. Tonight they come from across the ages. They too must enter the stable and speak of what they see. These too are witnesses. First comes the Artist.

The Artist

The barn is a bright poster paint yellow,
The woman an oily blue . . .
And her face as smooth as a silk screen,
As star dust ripples like water colour
Through unpainted gaps in the ceiling.
And in a cradle,
Propped up by stipple brushes,
Lies a pastel baby.
Blood splatters on the floor,
Like paint from an air brush.
And the soft pencil lines in Joseph's face
Change to a watery pink.
But as the baby cries, the colours run and distort,
And the painting transforms
Into the whirling, swirling, swishy-washy depths of the cleaning sink,
Where the colours run to the centre of the earth . . .
And to the end of the rainbow.

Barnaby Love, 13 years

Narrator: Next comes a schoolboy, restless for the holidays and dawdling on his way to school.

The Schoolboy

I enter the creaking door
And I step in some dung,
As brown as yesterday's toffee
Bought for a penny at the corner shop.
A spider, silvery as the shiny blade of my penknife,
Hangs on a silken thread.
A cow nuzzles my spine.
And, there in the manger,
Another squawking baby.
But he's smiling.
He reaches for me
And his radiant smile warms the stable.
His head is as shiny as the varnished conker
Which I used to beat Jack.
But his hands are the soft pink blankets
In which I sleep.
A cow burps . . .
How funny! How very comic!
And then a mouse scuttles across the earthen floor,
Under which lie strata . . .
We learned that in Geography today.
But now I'd better go,
Or I'll be late for school . . .
And it's nearly Christmas Day!

Alec Thomas, 12 years

Narrator: A poacher comes next. He has lain in the wet fields of the early
morning and heard the feather fall from the pigeon's breast and
smelled the breath of the hare, grass-sweet in the cold air.
Tonight he speaks of a stable.

The Poacher

The owl whispers to itself,
quietly, softly.
And I see a stable made of gun shaped beams,
loaded with strength and power.
A baby, plump as a pheasant chick,
but born in a stable,
where cobwebs hang like laced guitar strings,
spreading in every corner . . .
And the smell of steaming dung
mixes with mouse droppings
in the warm, soft hay.
A new beginning . . .
and a voice carried by the wind
breathes Christmas throughout the land.

Damian Thurlow, 12 years

Narrator: After the poacher comes the Gipsy. She too lives close to earth
and looks through the stable door in her own special way.

The Gipsy

The stable is . . .
A giant lantern.
Bitter smells of dung
Wisp free from the hay.
The oxen stand proud.
Mists of breath
Stream in rivers
From cooking pot nostrils.
A small drop of rose water
Lies still in a mother's arms,
His frog-soft body,
Pink,
Plump.
Egg-speckled hens

Scratch, contented, in the straw.
I can smell them already,
Stolen . . .
Roasting crisply
On ribbons of fire.
Strings of flies
Crawl like ivy
Over a cow,
Then settle on crusty stews of dung.
A colour splashed cat
Lies curled on the hay,
Like a rabbit
In a chamber of its burrow.
Its whiskers . . .
Are the strings of my violin,
Threaded tightly
Through its face.
I turn to leave,
Then stop.
And place my bunches of heather and herbs
In the straw.
A gift to the family.

Clare Watkinson, 12 years

Narrator: Then comes an actor. She has waited in the wings ready to make her entrance. But the scene has changed and she stands at the door of a stable. The play must go on.

The Actor

Red velvet curtains open on . . .
A wooden stable
Where a baby rests
In a bed of coarse and matted straw.
Oxen stand,
Like cardboard cut-outs
Which smell of powder paint and black markers.
A shepherd enters,
Cradles a stuffed lamb,
Whose eyes
Are two black buttons
Sewn on neatly with red thread.
But the lamb's nose
Is wet and runny as sweat.
The shepherd's eyes wander
The stable,
Blankly.
And the smell of . . .
Dusty costumes and make-up
Floats up,
And settles.
Then the red velvet curtains
Close
On a wave of clapping . . .
Then silence.

Lynne McLeod, 12 years

Narrator: Then the scene changes again. And a child takes the stage. She has come a long way and it is time to sleep. You see she has no story to tell. Unlike the others, she has never been to the stable and she does not know the Child. But as she sleeps she dreams. There is a Star and, in her dream, she follows it until she comes to a door. She opens it. Inside is the story she must tell.

The Amazing Birth

A splinter of bark
snaps off the wooden door.
As I lean on it,
I stare,
excited, yet patient.
A woman, sprawled on the floor,
eyes moist with anxiety,
heaves.
The cow's mouth hangs open,
like a foghorn . . .
and the moonlight pours through a hole
and shines on the baby,
like a spotlight.
His eyes sparkle
and his skin is warm and steaming
as dust falls from the roof,
like stars in a dream
to tangle with the cobwebs
which hang like chandeliers.
Everything is quiet,
until mice whisper,
echoing in the shed,
softly.
Does this child know
he is born to be King?

Emma Bicker, 12 years

Narrator: Then the witnesses rise, wake the Child, join hands across the
ages and the continents, and worship the King.

A Green Fable For Christmas

Traditionally, Christmas is a time when all earth rejoices. The rôle of the creatures has
been celebrated in story and song from Thomas Hardy's "The Oxen" in which the
beasts kneel at midnight on Christmas Eve to the story of the robin's breast scorched by
the flame of the stable fire. Here, in their verse drama "Seasons' Gifts", the Halesworth
children join that great company of storytellers and poets. A 'green' Christmas fable
cannot be didactic. It *can* acknowledge man's dependence on and respect for the natural
world and, most importantly, link wilderness and word at the moment when God
became Man and the word was made flesh. This time, unlike "The Reunion", there

was no costume, no movement: just children grouped on a dais to speak their own or other children's poems. Again, after the poems had been written within the set theme of "Seasons' Gifts", I provided the linking narrative and the dialogue between Sun and Moon.

Seasons' Gifts

Narrator: It was Christmas Eve and the Sun and the Moon met to decide what gifts they would bring the Child.

Sun: I have gold to give but my own great light cannot warm him this winter night.

Moon: I have silver to give but my own pale light is a cold welcome for the King of Kings on this winter's night.

Sun: We will call a meeting of the seasons. They have gifts in plenty to share with the newborn.

Narrator: First came Spring and as she spoke water ran from the frozen pond and the cuckoo sang in the fields as the leaves unfurled and earth grew green again.

Moon: What gift has Spring for the newborn?

Spring: I bring new life in the form of the dragonfly as it climbs from the mud into the world of air and clouds.

The Red Veined Dragonfly

The red veined dragonfly is . . .
A pen
With the nib as a tail
Lying on four
Tiny rings of paper
Covered in little red lines
Shining brightly,
His two cartridge ball eyes
And pencil lead legs
Floating through the air,
Gliding.
I watch him
Till he is out of sight,
Writing in the sky

That message . . .
He told me
How he had come from
A carcase
At the bottom
Of a deep dark swamp
And how he had
Fought his way through
Reeds and bulrushes
And met an army of
Waterboatmen
And had fought them,
Single-handed,
And been captured
And put in a mud cage.
How he had broken out
And swum to the surface.
Then flown off at top speed.
And how the brightness
Nearly blinded him.
But he had fought it.
And now he is
A silver knight
Fighting for the light
In the world of
Air and clouds.

David Whitehand, 11 years

Narrator: Then came Summer and as she spoke the warm waves ran on the sand, pigeons murmured in the cool of the forest and the corn grew tall in golden fields.

Sun: What gift has Summer for the newborn?

Summer: I bring a warm and midnight moment in the flight of the owl on its path to its hayloft home.

Owl at Midnight

As the moon glows
through the hatch,
it catches on the edges

of old forgotten farm machinery.
And then the ghost,
misty white.
His feathers are the furred lining
of the mouse's nest . . .
eyes like two great craters,
sunken in his full moon head.
He shuffles,
and then he takes off,
up to the rafters.
His outstretched wings
are the beams supporting
the skeleton of the barn.
And down again
to another beam,
landing softly.
A sudden "Gong"
of the church clock striking.
Twelve o'clock.
And he disappears again,
swallowed by the darkness,
off to his hayloft home.

Rebecca Howe, 12 years

Narrator: Then came Autumn and as she spoke the hare ran free over fresh
turned furrows, fires smoked in laden orchards and chaff hung
quiet in the mellow air. Everywhere was harvest.

Moon: What gift has Autumn for the newborn?

Autumn: I bring the wasps feasting on the windfall apple beneath the
laden tree and the flight of the swallow over harvested fields.

Migrating Birds

Lined up like paper clips on string,
Ready to be off.
The string bounces with tension.
And with a twang,
They fly . . .

And as the paper clips fall, they transform
Into a cloud of swarming bees.
Then, wings drop and they're
Arrows flying,
Shooting, stopping, starting,
As if chasing each other's tails.

Metamorphosis:
And they're swallows
Leaving.
They will not see
The harvesting of corn
From which each beak is made . . .
Or falling leaves,
Twisted, split and bent
which form each ragged body.

And as the sun grows red,
It roughens, reflecting in water
Where a bird scoops down to drink
And the mark of red spreads upon its chest.

Samantha Scriven, 12 years

Narrator: Last of all came Winter and as she spoke water stood still, the air
froze, and life hung in the balance between man and eternity as
the Word was made flesh.

Sun: What gift has Winter for the newborn?

Winter: I bring the great silence in which the Word is spoken. I bring a
donkey who carried a woman to Bethlehem, a fly on the wall of
a stable and the cry of a child on midnight air.

The Donkey

The donkey is an asthmatic pensioner
Puffing away the days
As though they were dandelion clocks.
Knife sharp teeth rotate,
Continually chewing.
He eats like a naughty child,
With his mouth open,

Slurping noisily.
The donkey is a docile creature
Plodding slowly along,
Comically waggling his baggy ears
Which are way out of proportion . . .
Like his live-in companion,
The rabbit.
The donkey's bulging eyes
Stare out from deep craters
In his lined old face.
He smells of last year's manure,
Old and musty,
As he flirts and flicks his long tail at an annoying fly,
Passing away the never-ending time
As though the days were dandelion clocks.

Catherine Ridley, 12 years

Just a Fly

The fly is . . .
A small wine stain
On a white tablecloth
That is quickly hidden,
Or disguised,
Balancing
On small stubs of pencil lead.
The wings are . . .
Two lacy curtains,
Flattened against the misty bathroom window,
And looking like a colours-by-numbers
That no-one has bothered to do.
Left to be . . .
Just meaningless lines
On a piece of paper.
It is a beggar,
A dirty tramp,
With nowhere in particular
To call its home.
Unnoticed,
Yet irritating,
Unheard,
Yet instantly seized upon
For its aggravating whispers.

Ugly,
Yet fascinating to observe and study.
It is a musical note,
Hopping from bar to bar,
Filling the page with rhythm and life.
And once, in the stable,
Long ago,
The fly settled on the donkey's tap shoe.
And watched the magical moment,
Paralysed,
With dreams
That mould and moult,
Violently swelling its tiny mind,
Until, a baby's cry awoke it,
And it became a charcoal chipping
Smudged against the barn,
Just a fly on the wall.

Jennifer Tracey, 13 years

Narrator: Then, the seasons rejoiced with the Sun and the Moon. And all
Earth worshipped the Child.

Winter Poetry

There is always some room for seasonal 'winter' poetry within a Christmas anthology where the emphasis is on the particular, the specific, the surprising image derived from the uniqueness of all personal experience. I have found Charles Tomlinson's "Winter Piece" a useful starting point because it is so closely observed and supplies vital moments of recognition and identification.

Winter-Piece

You wake, all windows blind – embattled sprays
grained on the mediaeval glass.
Gates snap like gunshot
as you handle them. Five-barred fragility
sets flying fifteen rooks who go together
silently ravenous above this winter-piece
that will not feed them. They alight
beyond, scavenging, missing everything
but the bladed atmosphere, the white resistance.
Ruts with iron flanges track
through a hard decay
where you discern once more
oak-leaf by hawthorn, for the frost
rewhets their edges. In a perfect web
blanched along each spoke
and circle of its woven wheel,
the spider hangs, grasp unbroken
and death-masked in cold. Returning
you see the house glint-out behind
its holed and ragged glaze,
frost-fronds all streaming.

Charles Tomlinson

Ted Hughes has written in *Poetry in the Making*:
"I doubt if much would come of just 'snow' as a subject. But there are an infinite number of categories within the general concept 'snow', and it is the teacher's job to help the pupil narrow the idea down to a vivid memory or fantasy."

So often the teacher's role must be that of a narrower down, rather than an opener up. Paradoxically, when the possibilities are narrowed down, they open up in remarkable ways. Always, imagination must be anchored in reality. That is where the excitement lies.

The Winter Seashore

Frost nipped at our ears and ankles,
Leaving them pinched pink.
We dodged tiny wet mirrors of water
And our mouths breathed eggs of steam.
Climbing the wet bank of sandy shingle was impossible.
Each footstep of sand tumbled down
And took you with it.
Then, at the top of the giant barricade,
The almighty mouth of water
That had swallowed sand and cliffs
And if we were not careful, it would swallow us.
And now, as I looked out to sea,
There was no skyline, just a vast palette of murky paint.
We walked, but the wind was so strong
That it blew us into a sidestep,
Then a lunge,
A sidestep, then a lunge,
A dislocated pattern.
This wind played games with our minds.
This sea,
Frosted in motion, took us in his hands,
And swallowed us.

Emma Buckingham, 12 years

Winter Churchyard

Not a churchyard,
A courtyard
Armed with white-wigged grave stones.
Silent with silence.
Their dirt grained faces
Stare with stiff necks
At one another,
Each one,
Guarded by its own bumped-up shadow.

The church's eye slit windows.
Lost,
Lost in the winter's white.
Its frost-frilled doorway
Peppered with boot grit,
Swimming in footprint puddles;
Escaping water hangs from the gutter
Caught in the cold,
Waiting for its freedom.
The sun pokes its head out
From the smoke-patched sky.
Unlocking the trees from their winter sentence.
For how long?

Oliver MacDonald, 13 years

Mastitis

How she suffers,
A cow.

When her udder is hard,
As cold as winter's web,

She strikes her calf away,
As it tries to suck,
Strikes, not meaning to hurt!

She bellows!

The icicles form on her breath.

Her udder bursts,
Rotted,
White milk flows,

Rapids on water.

She falls,
Sleeping death,
The ice overtakes her,
And the cold wind tears her away.

Marnie Smith, 12 years

Winter

A gull, its wings stiffly flapping,
Calls to a mate who'll never see home.
The landscape looks as if
Feathers by the million have fallen off a bird.
And a dead tree flowers again.
Flowers that no one can pick.

A goose, scrabbling frantically,
Falls through to abrupt silence.
And a sparrow hawk, so frail,
But made deadly with hunger,
Flicks along the hedgerow.

And last year's nettles,
Stork's legs in a sea of white,
Killed by the frost
While a swallow lies,
Dead and entombed in ice,
The perfect grave.

Matthew Line, 11 years

All the children's poems quoted in this section have been written for spoken performance. The sense of audience was immediate. Already accustomed to the idea of harness-
ing sound to meaning, this particular project provides a salutary experience of poetry in
performance. Sometimes a child revises his poem after rehearsal – redrafting with a
purpose. At other times when a child is speaking another child's poem there can be
useful collaboration between writer and speaker. Above all, the writing is seen to be
valued. There is response.

6 A Wizard of Earthsea

A Wizard of Earthsea is, first of all, an exciting, powerful story which children enjoy. It is also a parable of language which can form a proper basis of imaginative writing in prose and poetry. Like all parables or fables, it can be read at various levels; the most important level, however, is the story and related activities must not be tangential. (This would destroy the story's integrity by placing wrong emphases and distorting the themes.) In her essay 'Dreams Must Explain Themselves' Ursula le Guin herself says her novel is

> 'in one aspect, about the artist ... the artist as magician. The Trickster, Prospero ... Wizardry is artistry. The (novel) is then, in this sense, about art, the creative experience, the creative process.'

Certainly, *A Wizard of Earthsea* can be a powerful influence upon children's developing language awareness. It demonstrates the way in which language establishes identity, develops relationships and plays a vital part in the process of maturing. Ged, the young Mage, must face the pursuing Shadow which he himself has unleashed in the world; he must name it with his own name, and accept it as his darker self. Only then will he achieve integration and attain to maturity.

In another essay, 'This Fear of Dragons', Ursula le Guin makes this apology for fantasy:

> 'It is by such statements as "Once upon a time there was a dragon" or "In a hole in the ground there lived a hobbit" – it is by such beautiful non-facts that we fantastic human beings may arrive, in our peculiar fashion, at the truth.'

To read fantasy with children is to make no concessions to them. *A Wizard of Earthsea* will challenge and even frustrate at times; most importantly, it will give insight into the discipline of the poet's craft, the structure of his language, and identify the source of his inspiration.

The central theme of the novel is 'Naming'. This Naming emphasises the identity of the individual contained within the uniqueness of his first name. In *A Wizard of Earthsea* first names are magical, powerful, and conferred with ceremony. The boy Sparrowhawk receives his true name, Ged, at a baptism in the cold waters of the Ar. His name is known only to himself and his Namer, Ogion. It must be guarded jealously because to lose one's name into the hands of an enemy, is to surrender one's self.

All this has Biblical/historical undertones and is at odds with the casual modern indifference by which first names are such common currency that they are even displayed on car windscreens, easy prey to hostile forces lurking in hedgerow or ditch.

Ged is youthful, headstrong and reckless. His energy and enthusiasm rebel against tutor Ogion's gentle, yet rigorous training. Ged wants to work spells but has to learn names before he can aspire to mastery. Then, one day Ogion teaches him the name of the plant fourfoil. Naively, the apprentice asks what use it is. Ogion answers

> 'When you know the fourfoil in all its seasons root and leaf and flower, by sight and scent and seed, then you may learn its true name, knowing its being which is more than its use. What, after all, is the use of you, or of myself? Is Gont mountain useful, or the Open Sea?'

This is an articulation of the art of the poet. Only when we learn the true name of our subject, 'know its being', can we aspire to poetry. Moreover, we must 'know' through the senses

> 'by sight and scent and seed.'

Only then will the spell work, the poem say what we mean. Heather and Robin Tanner's book *Woodland Plants* complements this idea usefully and can be a legitimate digression. First, their commitment is impressive – a book started in 1939, laboured over for 42 years and finally published in 1981. Secondly, the informative text, balanced with meticulous drawings, communicates a true sense of 'knowing' by 'sight and scent and seed'. Drawings and text aspire to the truth of the creative artist. The exercise was costly.

At this point the children are able to attempt 'plant' poems, aware of the immensity of their task, yet hopeful of the potency of their craft. This is because they are working within the context of a literary/artistic experience; therein only can they find expression and release.

The Amaryllis

> The Amaryllis is . . .
> A tall tower with two trumpet flowers
> Bursting out of the top.
> The trumpets are as red as the sunset
> But not quite as shiny –
> They have not been polished.
>
> The stigma is like . . .
> An upside down drop of water frozen by time,
> The stalk a magnificent pillar,
> Growing so fast.
> Too fast,
> As fast as a fast forwarded video tape.
> It grows two inches a day.

Now the pillar stops growing.
But the trumpets push out, opening all the time.
The petals have glitter on them;
They look as though they have a skin of water.

The sunset trumpets finish opening.
Now they look as though
They are about to play.

William Mair, 10 years

Snapdragon

A frilled lip of gold, of gold dust falling from sunshine,
The puckered mouth of the silently angry dragon,
Wavering up on his green stalk tail,
Waiting.
Curl of scarlet velvet, his fire scorching the dust,
Licking the wall in a cluster of flames.
In cockerel comb splendour, the plump cushion
Is heavy. And the delicate neck is wrapped in wax paper
For protection.
A splash of rippling flag and he is crowned with gold fringing,
Triumphant but brooding.
He is a cavalier's doffed hat, flamboyant feather
Picked out in gold.
Battle colours charge the wind on a beige charger of lace,
His jousting pole, a beam of piercing sunlight,
Pretending to be jolly.
But the flushed skirt of rage does not fool anyone . . .
The tight collar strangling the light,
And the false smile, weatherbeaten into his lips.
The stem is strong green raffia,
But elastic, stretching further than it should,
So that when you pinch, he lurches to bite,
Clamping sour lips on flesh.
But the crusty dragon, old and lemon lipped
Cannot harm.
He has little perfume.
That which he has is stolen from the rose and dried.
In winter, he shrinks back
With rheumatism, his one master, the wind.
But always back in the summer.
A bumble bee, sensing blossoming danger,

Buzzes near and far.
The hum mingles with the hiss
Of wind on earth and leaves.
The hiss of the dragon.

Emma Walkey, 13 years

Bindweed

The bindweed rises from the nettles,
Climbing up the posts in a spiral.
Its twisted arms stretch up the fence.
It blooms pendants along the tread,
Making the old post
Into a maypole of flowers.
And a wire fence
Is solid again with wilted hearts
As it weeps for a loved one
In bursts of white handkerchiefs.
It follows the tracks of the wire.
In the damp morning
The bindweed clamps shut,
Opening into a windswept umbrella,
Catching the light,
Following its path,
Taking in its energy until . . .
Its rope stem clasps the flower,
Like a ring its gem.
And its leaves are ragged cat's ears.
The bindweed grows through the bush,
Like blood through the veins,
Layering the outside
In a progressive jigsaw.

Clair Honeywood, 12 years

Honesty

Papery, moth-like wings flutter in the wind.
The seeds are blackheads forming under the skin.
Ten or more silky moons on one twig,
each moon like a shooting star,
falling from time to time.
Bible-thin paper with no writing at all . . .

or an uninflated balloon, so thin,
With scrawled on eyes, nose and mouth.
And when it's June, it flowers
into purple and white shades cascaded everywhere.
Shaken, it sounds like mice across the floor,
the kind of sound people can't bear.
Newspaper flowers,
screwed up into shape,
perfect little flowers.
And then they change.
And they remind me of the time I went glass blowing . . .
light bulbs shining in the sun,
all shapes,
like bubbles stretched over rings . . .
and also cling film glistening.
An honest flower with no secrets,
hiding in corners of gardens.
But not hiding on purpose.

Anna Hursell, 13 years

Ogion's words about the fourfoil have a particular relevance for teachers today. This is a decade much concerned with 'usefulness'. Education must be relevant to industry, must be linked to the production and consumption needs of a technological society. Often the Arts may be accommodated only where they can demonstrate a dubious relevance to vocational training. Here Ogion gently questions such 'usefulness': the 'Being' of any person or thing 'is more than its use'. It is enough that it is. And all this within the context of a novel in which great deeds are enacted and a high value set on the common things of ordinary life: weatherworkers have a most practical rôle to play, binding spells make boats seaworthy, real wheatcakes are entirely preferable to meat pies which are mere illusion. Always, however, it is the wizard-artist who embodies the spirit of Earthsea. Art transcends 'usefulness' and any society which denigrates its wizard-artists loses its soul, and, paradoxically, its 'usefulness' at the same time.

Ged's precocity and the latent power within him chafe against the quiet tenor of his life with Ogion. Soon Ogion is forced to present his pupil with an ultimatum: learn to be silent with Ogion, 'the long road towards mastery,' or enrol as a pupil in the School for Wizards at Roke. Ged chooses Roke. Roke, however, selects its pupils carefully and entry is secured only when Ged is prepared to surrender his Name. Learning can take place only where there is trust and openness. Conversely, after having attained the status of Wizard, he is able to leave the school only when he asks the Doorkeeper his Name – to receive trust is an even greater responsibility and an essential part of the journey towards maturity. Here one child tries to express something about the nature of learning.

Student

> Through the sun dried branches
> I see the swallow fly.
> Unfaltering, curving and swooping,
> Bonded by instinct, in a way
> Unknown.
> Black across the sun,
> Diving down, down,
> Gliding through the hollowness,
> Fringed by white
> Through a gust and gone,
> Remembered only by the wind
> Buffeting its sharp passenger
> Along.
> The beauty of its being lithe and
> Taunting, for what is its beauty when
> Tethered?
> I, the swallow,
> Bound to this place,
> A great cavern of stone and magic.
> Warmer it gets now I have
> Intruded solemnly, to be placed
> In a world of learning,
> Appearing more forbidding
> As the ebbing tide of time
> Pushes by.

John Riches, 13 years

In this school all relates to Naming. At one point the students are sent to the Isolate Tower where they spend their time learning long lists of names:

'Magic consists in this, the true naming of a thing.'

The lists are endless. Language has infinite permutations and just as the wizard's task is hopeless, so is the poet's. Nevertheless

'A mage can control only what is near him, what he can name exactly and wholly.'

and the lists must be tackled. Always there is the incentive of the power that for Ged lies:

'like a jewel at the bottom of a dry well.'

These names are old; they have their sources deep within the culture of the people.

'Some names have been lost over the ages, and some have been hidden, and some are known only to the dragons and to the Old Power of Earth, and some are known to no living creature; and no man could learn them all. For there is no end to that language.'

There is mystery and excitement in these words which express man's ultimate aspirations, aspirations embodied in all Art, and here, most particularly, in poetry – the 'Naming' art of the wizard.

The Hardic language of Earthsea derives from the 'Old Speech'. Beginnings and roots are crucial. The way in which the Hardic language has developed from the metaphors of the 'Old Speech' demonstrates and clarifies the meaning of metaphor. Just as these metaphors of the 'Old Speech' are a more vital, more powerful language than the everyday Hardic Speech, so, for us, poetry is the most direct, strongest language of all when we want to say something important. Hardic *sukien* (foam) derives from the Old Speech *suk* (feather), *inien* (sea); ie, 'foam' is 'feather of the sea'. The need for exactness and appropriateness in metaphor is immediately apparent and the basis for work in which the children invent their own list of metaphors relating to the natural world. For example:

Wind – bed of the gull
        bird's rudder
        howl of the dying wolf
        husky breath of the giant
  Birds – feathered darts
  Ivy – Nature's scaffolding
  Snow – down of the goose
        fur of the snow seal
  Thunder – clapping of the winds
  Hail – peaks off mountains
  Bark – skin of a dead serpent

Lists appertain to the Isolate Tower and for a short while, as they coin these metaphors, the children take up residence there. In the Isolate Tower

    'It was cold and half-dark and always silent.'

While not cold and half-dark in the classroom, there is the relaxed silence of absorbed activity. *A Wizard of Earthsea* opens with a paradox:

        'Only in silence the word,
        Only in dark the light,
        Only in dying life,
        Bright the hawk's flight
        On the empty sky.'

Part of the tension of paradox is that it can only ever be partly resolved. Here, in experiencing something of the commitment of the poet, the children sense, at an intuitive level, that somewhere there is a resolution of all opposites, a harmony which is Truth. Wizards must aspire to it in their spells; poets in their metaphors.

I have found this work can be reinforced by a digression into Riddles. Although a digression, a study of Anglo-Saxon and modern Riddles can add another dimension to the reading, rather than compromise it. This is because a Riddle is a special kind of Naming. In a Riddle the name is secret (like so many true names in *A Wizard of Earthsea*). The poet alone knows the name hidden within the Riddle; his art is to reveal it to others through metaphor and to surprise while doing so. This word study is all the more potent because it derives from our culture. The condensed form of metaphor which was the Anglo-Saxon Kenning ('whale-road' for sea etc.) makes an appropriate introduction to Kevin Crossley-Holland's translations of Riddles: 'Pen and Fingers', 'Weathercock', 'Bellows', 'Anchor' and others.

Then there are the intriguing modern puzzles of May Swenson's *Natural Songs*. Children usually guess the 'answers' correctly and in their small success is a delight in realising the likeness between dissimilars. They are surprised – but only as they engage with the text as active readers. Excitement comes through a sharing of a secret which involves this special reciprocity between reader and poet. Then the roles are reversed and the children write their own Riddles. That is, they try to reveal the whole object by naming its parts in metaphor.

Smoke

The wistful figure
Dancing and prancing on the breeze.
The grey and ghostly
Haunting the rooftops,
The spirit of the warm and beautiful.

David Lawrence, 11 years

Pen

Light as a feather,
Going over the land leaving footprints.
One bony leg
Clambering over the hills, and jumping.
It has to be refilled
By blue rivers,
Making marks.

Caroline Smith, 10 years

The school in Roke deals in magic. Where there is magic, there must be rules. The rules are not articulated but rather implicit within the hierarchy of Archmage Nemmerle and the nine Masters whose business it is to educate the young mages. For instance, there is the matter of Equilibrium. The world is held in delicate balance and all wizards must be responsible in the way they exercise their power. Ged learns this lesson from the Master Changer who tells him:

'A wizard's power of Changing and of Summoning can shake the balance
of the World ... It must follow knowledge and serve need. To light a
candle is to cast a shadow.'

But Ged, who has wanted to change a rock into a diamond, feels dissatisfied with his Master's cautious wisdom. There is a parallel here with the Biblical story of the temptation in the Wilderness when Jesus was tempted to change a stone into bread. His refusal was a refusal to disturb the balance of the World, a respect for this Earth which transcended the gratification of his own needs. Children easily make these literary/ Biblical connections and through them are able to ask questions about the special responsibilities of modern scientists to maintain the balance of our world today. There is, however, no heavily didactic purpose in *A Wizard of Earthsea*. Rather, these issues give depth to an exciting story which has all the pace to hold attention to the end. Reading a novel like this teaches more about conservation than any amount of overt preaching. As Ursula le Guin says:

'fantasy is true'.

If the children are to assimilate and understand these basic themes of the novel, they must write and talk. One way is to adopt the role of Archmage Nemmerle and formulate rules for the school. Further, by articulating the roles, the children sometimes, unwittingly, say something about creative process. One child wrote this:

Rules for the School at Roke

Forget not The Creation of Éa for this shall be your strength through Good and Bad. Learn with whole heart and spirit.

1 Entry to the School of Roke shall be gained by placing your name, your true identity, in the doorkeeper's hands, and asking for help. Trust and humility form the key to enter the ivory tooth of the Great Dragon.

2 No changing spell may be locked. This is for the sake of Equilibrium, the balance of the world. To lighten the night is to darken the day.

3 Duels in sorcery are forbidden to all students at any time. Your fellow student is friend, not foe.

4 Spells, tricks, illusions, and other sources of magic and knowledge should be taught only by the mage concerned. Knowing the true name of a master is knowing how to end his life. Speak not his name, for this is his true identity.

5 Learn by whole heart the name, colour, scent, seed, life, death of each place, thing and being by the new day. Then the writing on the slabs shall be no more. The Isolate Tower is silent. Speak not within its walls. Time is sacred. Learn wholly and enjoy. The power you seek is like taking water from a spring, the tear duct of the planet.

6 The Immanent Grove is a place of enchantment. No spells are worked there. The trees are said to hold its powers. Speak not openly of its powers. At eighteen you may enter the Immanent Grove.

7 Leave the dead to lie in peace and tranquillity. Summoning of spirits is forbidden at all times. Danger could befall you, weakening your soul. My students, stay well away from this blackest magic.

8 Leaving the School of Roke is your final test. The tricks, illusions and power you have learned during your years you must now put to the test. Failure means staying at Roke until I see fit. Success means freedom is yours.

Choose well your path of life, my students, so that you grow wise and prosperous.

Signed: Archmage Nemmerle

Katrina Clouting, 13 years

Life in Roke is not always serious. The students are encouraged to play with and enjoy illusion. Although their work is rigorous and demanding, they find joy in it. A humourless Wizard would be a weak Wizard; a humourless poet, an ineffectual poet.

The chapter 'Iffish' provides another opportunity for legitimate digression. Vetch, Ged's great friend, has a sister Yarrow. Yarrow has no power but is curious. She asks Ged

'What other great powers are there beside the light?'
Ged replies

'It is no secret. All power is one in source and end . . . My name and yours, and the true name of the sun, or a spring of water, or an unborn child, all are syllables of the great word that is very slowly spoken by the shining of the stars. There is no other power. No other name.'

Again, this is to talk of our sources. And our own culture has the appropriate symbols:

'In the beginning was the Word.'

Within this literary experience these words have a special meaning for those concerned with the power of language. Richard Church, in his autobiography *Over the Bridge*, writes of their devastating effect when, as a boy in the classroom, he stumbled across them accidentally.

'I saw a new skyline defined. It was a landscape in which objects and words were fused. All was one, with the word as the verbal reality brought to material life by Mind, by man. It was therefore the very obvious, tangible presence of the Creator . . . I received a philosophy which I have never lost, a working faith in the oneness of all life . . . Everything was now contained for me, in the power of the Word.'

Richard Church himself admits that his response was over-literal, but, nevertheless, is quite sure of the authenticity of the experience. While it is unlikely that any of our children will have a Damascene literary experience of this kind, it is possible, that by considering our beginnings, they will make another of those connections within their culture and take another step on the road to language awareness. For example, our own Genesis story of creation read alongside some of the other great creation myths of the world, such as the Indian 'Shatarupa' provides a literary experience through which their understanding of the 'Word', as defined in *A Wizard of Earthsea*, is confirmed and deepened.

It is the Mage Ogion who defines the need for each person to attempt to come to terms with his beginnings if he is to grow to full maturity.

'a man would know the end he goes to, but he cannot know it if he does
not turn, and return to his beginnings and hold that beginning in his being.'

For us this is most possible within the structure of the received literary forms which are our particular heritage. We must know the great Creation myths of the World – our own especially. They are true in a special way; they embody each person's separate attempt to come to terms with his beginnings in order that he might know his end.

The children's attempts to articulate these beginnings must seem both audacious and stumbling within this context. They can be, nevertheless, necessary and authentic stages of language growth.

The Creation of the World

A child plays with his small red, blue and yellow ball. He throws it against the wall again and again and it rebounds every time like a piece of elastic springing back into place.

Now he kicks his ball high into the air. It falls straight down to land at his feet and again rebounds into the sky. He kicks it again. This time it does not fall at his feet but lands in a small stream.

It turns, twists and spins around, a small globe in the middle of a water universe.

The stones and pebbles, browns and blacks and whites mixed together are tiny planets around the small world. Slowly the current spins it around down the river of eternity.

A water lily for a sun. And the moon? A pure white feather, bent like a crescent, floats downstream.

The microbes in the water stick to the globe to form mindless beasts to live on this world in the infancy of its existence.

The End of the World

As the world drifts downstream it is punctured by the sharp edge of a flint. Now the small and colourful ball is twisted and wrinkled.

The little boy picks it up and slowly, sorrowfully, tears trickle down his cheeks. But his caring mother comforts him and from behind her back produces another blue, red and yellow ball.

Samantha Ellis, 13 years

Creation

Imagine . . .
Nothingness, blackness, non–life.
A single spark, light, as a
Moon starts a sun glowing,
Growing, winning its body by
A timeless dawn, the Alpha of
Omega, the grain of a mountain.
A world.
A spawn, an aspiring life roots
And begins. A movement.
The rustle, the learning spreads
As does the light.
It grows, multiplies;
Maybe a fish inheriting a past,
An eel or salmon but always
Life. Light.

John Riches, 13 years

Central to the novel is the search for one hidden name – the name of the Shadow unleashed by Ged. Until he can name the Shadow, it will roam Earthsea intent on working great evil, perhaps through Ged himself. The turning-point comes when Ged, refusing to run any longer, determines to hunt down his enemy and face it. Throughout, we have known the Shadow's name is a character in the novel and as the climax builds to the final confrontation, children speculate about its identity. Then comes the moment Ged and the Shadow speak the same name:

'Aloud and clearly ... Ged spoke the Shadow's name, and in the same moment the Shadow spoke without lips or tongue, saying the same word: "Ged". And the two voices were one voice.'

This is the moment of integration.

'Naming the shadow of his death with his own name, (Ged) had made himself whole: a man, who, knowing his whole true self cannot be used or possessed by any power other than himself, and whose life therefore is lived for life's sake and never in the service of ruin, or pain, or hatred, or the dark.'

And so, in naming and recognising the Shadow, Ged faces his darker self and in acknowledging this side of his nature attains to self-knowledge and freedom. He grows up. Ursula le Guin says in 'Dreams Must Explain Themselves'

'The most childish thing about *A Wizard of Earthsea*, I expect, is its subject: coming of age.'

She enlarges on this theme in 'This Fear of Dragons':

'maturity is not an outgrowing, but a growing up ... an adult is not a dead child, but a child who survived.'

By that criterion, many never attain to maturity. It is teachers' business at least to aspire to this for themselves and their pupils. Moreover, it is through developing language awareness, making the necessary literary connections, that self-awareness grows, develops into self-acceptance. Only then can we turn outward – articulate, expressive, whole.

Finally, Ursula le Guin's apology for fantasy (from 'This Fear of Dragons'). It is also, of course, an apology for English as a literature-based Arts subject in our schools.

'For fantasy is true, of course. It isn't factual but it is true. Children know that. Adults know it too, and that is precisely why many of them are afraid of fantasy. They know that its truth challenges, even threatens, all that is false, all that is phony, unnecessary, and trivial in the life they have let themselves be forced into living. They are afraid of dragons because they are afraid of freedom.'

7 The Poem and the Story

Childhood

I used to think that grown-up people chose
To have stiff backs and wrinkles round their nose,
And veins like small fat snakes on either hand,
On purpose to be grand.
Till through the banisters I watched one day
My great-aunt Etty's friend who was going away,
And how her onyx beads had come unstrung.
I saw her grope to find them as they rolled;
And then I knew that she was helplessly old,
As I was helplessly young.

Frances Cornford

My Grandmother

She kept an antique shop – or it kept her.
Among Apostle spoons and Bristol glass,
The faded silks, the heavy furniture,
She watched her own reflection in the brass
Salvers and silver bowls, as if to prove
Polish was all, there was no need of love.

And I remember how I once refused
To go out with her, since I was afraid.
It was perhaps a wish not to be used
Like antique objects. Though she never said
That she was hurt, I still could feel the guilt
Of that refusal, guessing how she felt.

Later, too frail to keep a shop, she put
All her best things in one long narrow room.
The place smelt old, of things too long kept shut,
The smell of absences where shadows come
That can't be polished. There was nothing then
To give her own reflection back again.

And when she died I felt no grief at all,
Only the guilt of what I once refused.
I walked into her room among the tall
Sideboards and cupboards – things she never used
But needed; and no finger-marks were there,
Only the new dust falling through the air.

Elizabeth Jennings

Again, it is the words of the poets which release memory and are a powerful motivation to write. In this case, Frances Cornford's "Childhood" was the impetus for some of the poems by younger children (9 – 11 years), and Elizabeth Jennings' "My Grandmother" for some of the poems by older children (11 – 13 years).

Because these are poems about people, for the most part, they arise out of anecdote. We all share a natural curiosity about people, sometimes expressed through unstructured gossip, occasionally through structured story, and, rarely, through the discipline and craft of poetry. Any encounter with a person is important because it may initiate a relationship, and a relationship implies a 'knowing'. We learn to 'know' a person only in part by looking; a poem comprising a list of physical details, however finely perceived and sensitively selected, may well end up by being clinical and inhuman. There must be an attempt to capture something of the mystery of human personality in all its elusiveness.

There is, for instance, Lara, who for years had watched two old men watching her as she ran in and out of her gate, played in her garden. The two old men were well known locally. Her poem drew an excited response from her class. Those same old men had sold roller skates with no buckle fastening to one girl's brother. He still felt cheated. There was reminiscence, convivial conjecture. But the poem made a difference. Lara had reflected on the old men's lives and had made connections within her own life. Most importantly, she had found words which transcend sentimentally to achieve an understanding which is the basis of true knowledge.

Sat on the Wall

They spent hour after hour,
Day after day,
Year after year
Sat on the wall.

One,
Thin and frail-looking.
Long chicken neck
Sprouting up from the faded collar
Of his whipped-up shirt.
His eyes,
Short-sighted slits
Swollen round the edges like pink puff-balls,
Lost in the stubby bristle of his face.
The other,
Plump, like a puffed-out cockerel.
His face,
Wrinkled like apple peel
On a compost heap.
Torn nets of burst veins
Knotted in reds and blues
Round his cheek bones,
Overcast by the shadow
Of his flat cap.

They sat on the wall,
Staring in bewilderment at me playing swingball.
Remembering
How once they amused themselves
Throwing pebbles at tin cans.
They sat,
Pondering over the differences
Between their childhood
And mine.

The frail one held tight
To the lead of an old dog,
Which nosed between his legs,
Pining for attention.
The other
Shuffled the dust
With the toe of his boot
And leaned with clasped fingers
On his walking stick . . .
For year after year,
Sat on the wall.

Then,
The frail one died.
And I never saw the other again.
The plump one never
Sat on the wall.
It wasn't the same
Without his friend . . .

Lara Mair, 12 years

Then there is Paul's response to the birth of his sister. In one sense birth is a commonplace; in another sense, it is a miracle. Here, as Paul holds the newborn and looks with the eye of the poet, he is utterly absorbed. Later, he remembers, reflects, and crafts his poem with all the necessary detachment. And then this birth, this commonplace is transformed into miracle.

Rachel   I gaze down.
Her large, midnight blue eyes stare back;
No tears when she cries.
Her arms wave about,
Fingers opening and closing like sea anemones
On the seashore,
With fingernail pearls on the end of each finger,
Shining in a cluster.
Hair sticking up,
But not untidy,
Just fuzzy,
Masses of it,
Completely covering her tiny head.
Her small rosebud mouth,
Blowing up an imaginary balloon,
Seems to smile,
Then laugh,
Almost shape up to whistle.
Her fascinating face is chubby,
Lively,
But peaceful.
Gown far too big,
Spindly arms and legs sticking out.
She doesn't cry.
My four hour old sister
Is contented,
Lying in my arms.
I hug her close,
My lovely sister.

Paul Sparkes, 12 years

Ben attempts to capture the pain of first love in his words. This is probably possible only from the detached viewpoint of six years later when he can look back with a certain wry humour. Again this is a matter for laughter and reminiscence as 13 year old Kirstie finds her 7 year old self celebrated in a poem.

First Love

School! . . . a strange place.
Love! . . . even stranger.
Kirstie Leeming . . . six years old,
yet a real shocker.
Pigtails like silky hemp
wrapped around two pieces of wire
held together by two red ribbons.
She would parade around the playground,
like a model on the catwalk.
Five year olds would stare.
Eight year olds would wolf whistle.
And teachers would sigh.
She wasn't at all boastful or proud,
but considerate and happy,
like a dizzy ballerina.
I adored her at primary.
I would sit staring at her, dreamily . . .
a drunken bat flying into the moon.
Until I was woken by my friend's elbow,
as the teacher passed.
Michael Aldridge stood in my way.
He was like the Berlin Wall;
I was West Germany;
and Kirstie was East Germany.
But those times are long gone
and the wall has come down.
Kirstie and I are older.
And just friends;
all is just memories
of primary days long gone.

Ben Northover, 13 years

In the next poem Grandad appears only in the title; and yet his presence and his relationship with his grandson are most surely communicated.

Mole Trapping With Grandad

The heavy thump of hobnail boots
And the sharp retort
As a moling-stick strikes a flint.
You can feel the soft lack of earth
As you push a stick
With a quick jerk into a tunnel . . .

Then, the grind of the jaws
As they slowly open and click into place.
Tiny droplets of dew
Slide off the grass
As the turf is lifted
And the trap is slowly pushed in.
And you catch a whiff
Of stale air as it forces its way out.

Then sitting, after setting a good number of traps,
Under my favourite oak,
Eating a packed lunch,
And leaning back to look at nests
As they sway and rock in the wind . . .
I wonder if they get seasick.

Then, it's back off to the well remembered spot
To dig up the trap, to see a dead mole,
A cold, forgotten pair of ear muffs,
Lying limp in my hands.
I suddenly push it into the bag.
I shrug and tell myself,
Never again.

Matthew Line, 11 years

If birth and love are commonplaces to everyone except the family and the afflicted, death remains more than ever the great taboo. In the next poem Darren remembers the day he saw a man drown. Economy of expression and the delicate understatement of the ending are the hallmarks of authenticity. For me the ending carries echoes of John Donne's words:

'No man is an island entire of itself . . . any man's death diminishes me, because I am involved in Mankind. And therefore never send to know for whom the bell tolls; it tolls for thee.'

Of course, Darren does not yet know these words. But he has discovered their meaning. This discovery was made not at the moment when he was moved almost to tears on the river bank, but in the quiet moment of reflection and withdrawal when the poem was written.

The Drowning

On the river opposite –
A man in a canoe.
Down the rapids he went
Faster than an arrow.
He knuckled against a rock.
He capsized.
He slammed his head on the bottom
And stayed there.
Unconscious.
I sat, hoping he would surface.
Quickly,
The lifeguard slicked into the river.
Later . . .
The man lay there,
A dead salmon.
His friend cried.
And I who didn't know this man
Cried . . .
A little.

Darren Feller, 12 years

Nicholas

Nicholas is small to the onlooking world,
a frail miniature child,
but inside,
energy overflows
and his mind strengthens from day to day.

His small roundish face
is alight with a smile
which seems to be
four sizes too big for his mouth.
His ears,
almost pricked like a dog's,
waiting for the faintest noise.

His foot, bent, stiff
as if frozen,
ready to kick the ball.

His eyes stare
solidly, but almost delicately,
full with concentration,
aiming to hit the ball.

His foot swings
like a clock's pendulum.
The foot makes contact
and the ball bobs
for a short distance
like a car
using up the last drops of petrol . . .
Then it stops.

His face screws up
with disgust
like a shrivelled apple.
He turns
and starts running on his short stout legs,
almost like a partridge.

Robert Adcock, 11 years

Grandad

Grandad smelled of fish boiled in milk
And liquorice root on which he continuously chewed,
Grumbling about taking pills,
Although they were all that kept him alive.

There was a pile of pipe cleaners
By the fireplace
Smelling of dust
And used too many times,
Like the bleached chicken bones
On the birdtable.

He had been working on the allotment
In his better trousers
So they got muddy

And he had scrubbed them
With a wire brush.
Then had to try and darn them again.

The hardened globule of denture cream
Looked like birdsplash
On the side of the vase,
In which flowers melted into the water,
Staining the glass at the waterline.

When I was very small
There was always a toy phone
On which we played a game
In which he ordered sacks of potatoes.
So I used to bring them round,
Out of the garage.
He gave me 5 pence per sack.

Then he died,
Mixing with smells
Of camomile tea
And boiled fish.

Edward Line, 13 years

The Old Lady

The day we went bob-a-jobbing
We met her.
She sat there
In a dainty old chair.
She never moved,
Her faint white hands
Perched on the chair
Like two shot birds.
She was wrapped head to foot
In blankets and shawls
As if she was a hermit crab
In her neutral home.

Wrinkles curved over her soft face
As if a snail had left its trail.
She opened her mouth
And mumbled, "Hello".

She looked pleased with herself,
Like a child who had just
Learnt to write her name.
Her hair –
What was left of it –
Looked like tiny spiders' webs
Knotting all over.

She took my hand
As if to say, "Come closer".
She felt my face
As if wondering whether to buy me or not.
She clutched my hand harder,
Then let go.
I sniffed a pricey perfume
Over her clingfilm skin.
Then with a great sigh
She leaned back into her chair.
I knew then, it was time to go.

Robert Adcock, 11 years

Great Uncle: The Death of a Friend

His face was like tired paper,
Creased and dirty;
He did not wear his cap then
As he always used to
And his bald head was so rosy
I could have eaten it.
National Health glasses
Propped on a run-of-the-mill nose
And hooked around
Ears of stamped clay.
His eyes were those of a young lion
Pawing through the bars of age,
Yearning for hedge and field,
Wood and stream.

We talked about life,
Though he was closer to death.
Close to death . . .
But still the urge for life.
He needed no charity;
No home would have held him.
Not this lion.
A hospital? Pah!
For the sick.
Weak in body,
His mind took him
Places beyond himself,
Even in his boyhood.
Now only hospital could hold his mind.
And it did.
One week in hospital
Tamed the lion,
Cut hedge and wood,
Ploughed the field . . .
And he died.

Clifford Black, 13 years

8 Water

Personal Helicon

As a child, they could not keep me from wells
And old pumps with buckets and windlasses.
I loved the dark drop, the trapped sky, the smells
Of waterweed, fungus and dank moss.

One, in a brickyard, with a rotted board top.
I savoured the rich crash when a bucket
Plummeted down at the end of a rope.
So deep you saw no reflection in it.

A shallow one under a dry stone ditch
Fructified like any aquarium.
When you dragged out long roots from the soft mulch
A white face hovered over the bottom.

Others had echoes, gave back your own call
With a clean new music in it. And one
Was scaresome for there, out of ferns and tall
Foxgloves, a rat slapped across my reflection.

Now, to pry into roots, to finger slime,
To stare, big-eyed Narcissus, into some spring
Is beneath all adult dignity. I rhyme
To see myself, to set the darkness echoing.

Seamus Heaney

Death of a Naturalist

All year the flax-dam festered in the heart
Of the townland; green and heavy headed
Flax had rotted there, weighted down by huge sods.

Daily it sweltered in the punishing sun.
Bubbles gargled delicately, bluebottles
Wove a strong gauze of sound around the smell.
There were dragon-flies, spotted butterflies,
But best of all was the warm thick slobber
Of frogspawn that grew like clotted water
In the shade of the banks. Here, every spring
I would fill jampotfuls of the jellied
Specks to range on window-sills at home,
On shelves at school, and wait and watch until
The fattening dots burst into nimble-
Swimming tadpoles. Miss Walls would tell us how
The daddy frog was called a bullfrog
And how he croaked and how the mammy frog
Laid hundreds of little eggs and this was
Frogspawn. You could tell the weather by frogs too
For they were yellow in the sun and brown
In rain.

Then one hot day when fields were rank
With cowdung in the grass the angry frogs
Invaded the flax-dam; I ducked through hedges
To a coarse croaking that I had not heard
Before. The air was thick with a bass chorus.
Right down the dam gross-bellied frogs were cocked
On sods; their loose necks pulsed like sails. Some hopped:
The slap and plop were obscene threats. Some sat
Poised like mud grenades, their blunt heads farting.
I sickened, turned, and ran. The great slime kings
Were gathered there for vengeance and I knew
That if I dipped my hand the spawn would clutch it.

Seamus Heaney

This topic may be introduced with readings of two 'water' poems by Seamus Heaney which I have found work well with twelve to thirteen year olds. It is commonly argued that to ask a child to write a poem immediately after having read one is to debase the original work and, more importantly, to preclude enjoyment. I have found, however, that it is immediately after having made a literary connection within a text that a child finds that he has something worthwhile to say. Again, it is a matter of excitement. Recognitions are exciting and need articulating. The moment of identification can become an expressive moment if an area of experience has been defined in a new and surprising way.

The first poem, 'Personal Helicon', is a return to the childhood fascination with water. This is to return us, through the minutiae of the memories, to our own beginnings. First, there is the specific naming of 'pumps', 'buckets', 'windlasses' – concrete, unadorned 'naming'. Then, the hint of mystery, the sinister undertone in 'dark drop', 'trapped sky'. The poem is heavily sensuous and therefore deliberately evocative. There is a dwelling on the smells, the sounds, the textures:

'the smells
Of waterweed, fungus and dank moss . . .
I savoured the rich crash when a bucket
Plummeted down at the end of a rope . . . '

Most importantly, echoes and reflections run throughout. To a child, an echo or reflection is a fascinating affirmation of self, almost an image of the self-knowledge which lies tantalisingly just around the corner. It is, above all, a matter for play and experiment; sometimes, as in stanza 4, for fearful experiment.

'And one (well)
Was scaresome for there, out of ferns and tall
Foxgloves, a rat slapped across my reflection.'

Foxgloves are poisonous; there is also the aggressive assonance of 'rat slapped'. And our vulnerable, curious self is threatened. The quest for knowledge of the world and our own place in it is a dangerous quest. Similarly, the work of the poet in stanza 5 is no less fearful, needs no less temerity. The childish play and experiment is over and now

'I rhyme
To see myself, to set the darkness echoing.'

These twelve to thirteen year olds are at a moment in their lives when they are particularly receptive to this poem. They have a foot in both worlds. They still play and experiment in an entirely childlike way but they are also becoming young adults, capable of the poetic detachment which will set their own darkness echoing. They have, at the same time, the poet's and the child's apprehension of 'reflection'. Looking at a reflection is introspective; there must now be a turning outwards, if a poem is to be written. The inevitable question follows: where is your own 'Personal Helicon'? This question is an especially authentic starting point for children's writing. The connection with the Greek Muses confers a special importance on the task. There is no point in writing about anything unless it is important (although paradoxically, of course, it can be only the act of writing which makes a matter of this kind important). Thereby the writer attains to self-respect as well as self-knowledge.

Read alongside this poem, 'Death of a Naturalist' adds another dimension. Again the poet returns to childhood and so his subject is easily accessible to children. In rank, sensuous imagery Seamus Heaney paints a picture of the festering flax dam and his boyhood fascination with:

'the warm thick slobber
Of frogspawn that grew like clotted water.'

Then there is the cosy familiarity of the classroom world where Nature is contained within jam jars and Miss Walls reduces all to Nursery dimensions.

'Miss Walls would tell us how
The daddy frog was called a bullfrog
And how he croaked and the mammy frog
Laid hundreds of little eggs and this was
Frogspawn.'

There is the comfortable folklore of
'You could tell the weather by frogs too
For they were yellow in the sun and brown
In rain.'

Then the conversational rhythm breaks. There is the ominous, heavy tread of syllables in
'Then one hot day when fields were rank'
and we come upon the tough, primitive reality which is poetry. Miss Walls' jam jar of sentimentality cracks – her cosy classroom world plays the boy false when he is confronted by the angry, invading frogs:

'their loose necks pulsed like sails. Some hopped.
The slap and plop were obscene threats. Some sat
Poised like mud grenades, their blunt heads farting.'

And the 'naturalist' within the little boy dies as he sickens, turns and runs.

Obviously much remains to be said about both these poems but these are readings for children, designed only to send them back to their own experience with a sense of discovery and importance. Each of the following poems was written after these two readings. In no way do they 'copy' Seamus Heaney (that would indeed be to debase his work). Rather, the professional poet has helped them to re-visit a watery place and recapture its atmosphere through the feelings associated with it.

The Terrapin

His tortoise-shell back, a barnacle
Clutching at the painted algae.
His pipe-cleaner neck rigid,
His lonely head shunts to one side, staring into nothing,
The lamp-lit world empty without his shy companion.
His grim features seem to say,
'Where's my friend? Where's my brother?'
He rolls into the water
And attacks his reflection in the glass.
As the gravel swirls, sand storms arise –
Now the tank is a smoke sheet, a creeping fog.
Then – out of the mist, a prehistoric fossil clambers to its rock
To wait alone for its own end.

Matthew Shepherd, 11 years

River Blyth

In the summer I waded the Blyth.
Slipping on muddy flints,
I travelled the length of the river.
At one point,
Baby eels sucked at my toes
And tiny water spiders secretly
Hid between specks of sand.

On and on
The soft mud
Grudgingly let my walking stick
Sink into its oozy layers.

Then – a reed laced with dirt
Where a kingfisher
Dashed nearby into
The murky below
And caught a minnow.

On under the bridge
Where nothing grew,
Except slippery slime.
Flounders scudded
As I kicked duckweed.

I clambered up the sun-baked river bank.
Pieces of earth
Crumbled like a biscuit
Into the water below.
Satisfied,
I made my way home.

Matthew Watson, 13 years

Our Pond

In one corner,
under the paving,
lives a grass snake;
he looks like a creased-up old drinking straw
and swims around
eating the pondskaters,
scraps of tinfoil,
frail and easily broken.

Newts live in that pond;
they are lazy,
sun-worshipping sticks;
Any movement,
and each stick finds legs and dashes to safety.

The water snail,
living in hermit fashion,
and coated with algae,
wants only the peace and quiet to eat his meal.

The goldfish,
a lazy mass of flesh poised between life and death,
is still like a picture.

Our pond is a natural habitat;
man, an outsider:
Please leave Nature at work.

Russell Wood, 12 years

The River

The clear, slow-running river
is a two-way mirror.
Fish stare up at me
through my reflection.

A kingfisher,
a spectrum of colours,
perched on an overhanging tree,
studies the still waters,
its beak a sharpened spear-head.
A silver torpedo
fins past.
A flash of blue spark,
a dart in the bull's-eye.
An orange-peel sunset
lies on the water.
Coke cans and
brown crisp packets
bob up and down like plastic ducks
on the scarlet mirror.
A running stream of warm blood.

As I stand back, knee-deep
in the deathly silence,
only the ripples slapping
against my boots,
fear rises in my throat,
a weird feeling.
Through the nettles and brambles
I pull my boots
from the black oozing mud –
and run.

Malcolm Goodwin, 13 years

Tree Collection

Rainwater,
Collected in the stump of a three-way tree,
Ripples
Like a transparent blanket
Shaken between two people;
Only no dust is blown up.
Tiny fragments of bark falling,
Like melted icicles,
Gently slide into the water.
The specks rock back and forth, like a cradle,
As they slowly sink down.
As the wind drops,
An autumn leaf floats on the surface,
Its once crispy skin,
Soggy,
Like clothes soaking in the kitchen sink.
A beetle comes crawling down the trunk,
As if stalking a life or death prey.
A metallic spectrum
On its jet black back
Glitters in the sun.
I listen hard;
The wind is rustling the first leaves of spring,
A mother soothing her baby.
No other sound;
The whole world seems to be silent for me,
Just how it should be,
As I gaze into my miniature universe.

Lara Mair, 10 years

Stillness

The water is still,
Except for a trickle of breeze
Through the curving willows.
A piece of crust
Left by the flustering ducks,
Drifts gently out
Like a graceful swan.
Mud stirs,
And the crust is suddenly immersed
In a battle of swirls and swells.
They stop.
And a fanned out fin
Breaks the surface.
Then comes a telescopic mouth,
And with a suck and a gargle
The crust is gone with the great carp
To the decaying bottom.
An angler whips his fine tackle
Out to the quivering reeds,
While a timid water-vole
Scurries through the overhanging grass
And into the water.
His ripples die
And sink.
The water is still.

Jamie MacDonald, 12 years

That Pond!

Swiftly gliding about,
Suddenly tipping up a little,
The water making a V shape after the boat.
We were screaming for joy.
Then, turning around and heading for the shore,
Elizabeth gradually stepped out.
I wanted to go with her,
Like a little child wanting to go with her mother.
I was about to step when . . .
Elizabeth shouted, 'Hang on!'
Too late . . .
I fell in.
Haah!

Help!
Splashing about.
The taste of the slimy dirty water,
The ducks flying out of the way,
Their wings spread,
And shouting that they had been disturbed.
Elizabeth slowly hauled me out.
Standing on the shore dripping wet,
The squelchy feeling of water in my boots,
Like a soggy squelchy jellyfish.
I ran home
And went into my bedroom crying.
Then – feeling of clothes
And warm air around me.
I felt glad to be at home –
But
That pond!

Rosalind Roberts, 11 years

Canal

Jumping on the stone slabs,
I balance on one leg.
I wobble,
    stumble,
        then fall.
It is cold.
My head goes under and I cannot see.
The thick surface reflects the sun,
And looks like tinted glass.
The wall of the canal is covered
With a tapestry of slime,
Wet leaves woven together with hair.
My shoe comes off
And my foot strokes the bottom;
The mud is warm to my toes
And floats to the surface, like strands of smoke.
Air bubbles, too, rise like transparent balloons,
Only to pop at the surface.
And water floods through my clothes
And weighs me down.
Kicking and spluttering,
I rise to the surface, hold my breath,

And sink back down again.
Then up like a yo-yo.
I am hauled to land like a captured fish.
But now I can breathe.
The water is still
But a murky patch pollutes the dank surface
And swirls in endless patterns
To settle on the bottom, in my lost shoe.

Sally Clifton, 12 years

A return to some of the 'sea' prose pieces in the Journal of Gerard Manley Hopkins was the starting point of some 'sea' poetry linked to the 'water' theme. Again, the imagery demonstrates the individuality of the response;

'And there are channels,
Like the veins of a clipped pony's neck'

could be written only by a child who has worked with horses and has made a particularly arresting connection with another area of her experience – the seashore. The image is new, surprising, and was released through a close reading of some prose pieces by Gerard Manley Hopkins. These pieces made her own experience important and worth writing about.

Seaside Show

Sea surf trickles;
Water ripples scurry to the sand,
Leaving spidery channels
Like a small child's writing.
Scuffing shoes.
One stone,
Speckled like a thrush's breast.
A hidden vacuum sucks at my boot.
A seagull screams overhead,
Protesting it seems.
I scrape a stone along the sand
And there are channels
Like the veins of a clipped pony's neck.
Pom-pom creatures bristle,
Red silk waves.
Tentacles plunge;
And then all is calm.
Only the gentle splish splash of the sea.

Ruth Hooton, 12 years

Washed Up

A yard of fishing net,
torn rope hugging the silt,
an empty oil drum beating
to the sound of waves.
Jellyfish, stodgy cake mix,
rotting in the sun.

A bar of driftwood
scrawls tiny ditches
on the sand;
the brine seeps
into caves in the wood
and flakes off splinters
on to the moist sand.

An oil-sodden seagull
is tarred to pebbles
and is dead as a wall.
Its liquorice body ruffles
in the bite of the wind.

Bulbs of seaweed
scratch against golden sand
and quiver as the tide nears,
spewing out froth as it comes.
The seaweed disappears
under a mass of water once more.

The tide ebbs
and the treasure trove of debris
moves out to the deeps,
again.

Matthew Goddard, 13 years

Rock Pool

Rock pool, rock pool,
See the sand guzzle
The sour sea.
Each drip of water,
Tasteless and dry.
A swirl of sand rubs
Between my toes,
Worms wriggling.
Faint echoes of ships' horns
Blowing
And the rock pools humming.
A small crab,
Its legs long, thin.
Its eyes,
Sizes of melon pips.
I touch the crab's shell.
Hard but breakable,
It looks like a soft green lily top.
A pebble lies crushed,
Smashed against the tide's
Pestle and mortar,
And now
The pebbles are the sands.

Michelle Saunders, 13 years

Story can also be a sound basis for poetry writing. Obviously the story must be sufficiently well known for the poem to read well out of context. An excellent source of such stories is the Bible. The two 'watery' stories 'Noah's Ark' and 'Moses in the Bulrushes' were the background for the poems which follow. As with the Christmas writing, the aim was to give an old story new relevance and impact. These two stories seem less likely to evoke stereotyped images, perhaps because we do not celebrate them. Nevertheless, they are deeply woven into our culture and the kind of story we feel we always knew. A good starting point for the 'Noah' story is Judith Nicholls' 'Japheth's Notes – A Fragment'. The title itself asserts a new reality, while the images are sensuous and conceived within the terms of the writer's experience – so they make the story new.

'First waterdrops
on father's upturned head,
dew on a web of thinning hair . . .
Nostrils sharp with gopher wood and pitch.'

This is, above all, an attempt to answer the question 'What was it really like?' This is a challenge to the imagination and, again, it can be met only within the writer's memory. Indeed it is only as the old story makes connections within the experience of each generation that it works as a story. A poem about that story must arise out of those personal connections. Moreover, the Ark is a particularly appropriate subject for poetry as it is itself a poetic symbol. Each animal aboard the ark was one particular creature which had attained universality. The cows, for example, were two unique creatures which nevertheless represented all cows everywhere. This idea builds on and extends the work done on the children's 'Thought-Creature' poems. It forms for them another layer of poetic experience.

Noah's Ark

The cow's body
like a map,
the giraffe's neck
like a ladder.
The monkey's ears
ready to take off.
And Noah's print
in cow's dung
like a big black hole
drying fast.
The spiders in the corner
spinning their
riches of wet pearls.
The elephant wrinkled
like a closed-up hand.
The parrot talking,
performing its act.
The apes' holloas
like foghorns.

While outside
the sea is drowning
and the ark riding its waves.

Emma Smith, 13 years

The Great Flood

The meadow now a painter's palette;
Bulrushes, escaped bristles from a brush,
Drowning in paint, drowning in water.
A blind-witted hedgehog trundles to its death,
Sinks, leaving tips of spikes as floating gold dust.

A tree's roots turn into dead man's fingers,
Wilting to soft decaying pulp.
Like a lost child, a starling,
Clenching to a rock,
Cries out to the sky.
For help?

The meadow is now the weighted wings
Of a frail butterfly;
Straining with no energy,
Straining to keep above the surface.

The butterfly sinks as the water rises.

Gail Bloomfield, 13 years

Noah's Ark

The ark, the one and only.
Stories, pictures . . . can't imagine how big it really was . . .
How terrifying that first raindrop that fell,
The first haynet which was filled
Full of sweet-smelling hay,
Caught in our terrified minds like smoke.
The loneliness of a cow, missing her calf,
Stands desolated in a corner.
Pigs grunt, groan;
They do not show their loneliness; their hearts are strong.
I walk to the stall. A muzzle gathers on my hand.
Then . . . they all sleep.

When that first and last raindrop fell . . .
How wonderful to have seen through that terrible storm.
Stories, pictures . . . can't imagine how bad it really was . . .
How wonderful that last raindrop that fell,
The last haynet filled.

Sarah Wright, 12 years

Fate

Mud rises like a chiffon scarf
dancing with green slime partners;
a smell of sickness.
A tarred basket made from reeds.
Containing what?

I peer in and see a bundle,
two dark eyes peering into a forest of bulrushes
and a mouth opening and shutting
while the body struggles,
restless in the bands of linen.
The water settles.
But the dying and killing
Never stop.

Caroline English, 13 years

The Ark

I am the ant,
The ant who boarded the world
In fright at the first drop of rain
That could kill me.
I am the ant.
My memory reflects in outside worlds
Of sweetmint air.
Now,
The smell of sweat and dung decayed.
My small body hides
Where an elephant stamped impatiently
And where a man crouched under creaking bows,
Clasped hands together and prayed.
A drop of rain
And my unbelief surrenders.
And then the motion of sadness;
The rank smell of fresh gopher wood fills me.
Yet worse –
My tiny nostrils sense stricken panic
From the outside world.
The stretch of water is endless
And already
Bodies of black and white rhinos,
Bloated with water,
Clot the surface
And a layer of insects smothers,
A covering for the already dead.
I crawl inside
And sit in a crevice
Watching the destruction
While forty days and nights pass on.
Then the dove gives thanks:
The world,
Two of each,
Will live on.

Charlotte Hawthorn, 13 years

9 Thresholds

"They were at the foot of the Mound.

'How do we get in?' said Roland.

'Through the door.'

'What door? It's just turf.'

'That is why you are here,' said Malebron. 'The door is hidden, but you can find it.'

'How?' said Roland.

'Make the door appear: think it: force it with your mind. The power you know fleetingly in your world is here as real as swords. We have nothing like it. Now close your eyes. Can you still see the Mound in your thought?'

'Yes.'

'There is a door in the Mound,' said Malebron. 'A door.'

'What kind of door?' said Roland.

'It does not matter. Any door. The door you know best. Think of the feel of it. The sound of it. A door. The door. The only door. It must come. Make it come.'

Roland thought of the door at the new house. He saw the blisters in the paint, and the brass flap with "Letters" outlined in dry metal polish. He had been cleaning it only yesterday. It was a queer door to be stuck in the side of a hill.

'I can see it.'

'Is it there? Is it firm? Could you touch it?' said Malebron.

'I think so,' said Roland.

'Then open your eyes. It is still there.'

'No, it's just a hill.'

'It is still there!' cried Malebron. 'It is real! You have made it with your mind! Your mind is real! You can see the door!'

Roland shut his eyes again. The door had a brick porch, and there was a house leek growing on the stone roof. His eyes were so tightly closed that he began to see coloured lights floating behind his lids, and they were all shaped like the porch entrance. There was no need to think of it now – he could see nothing else but these miniature, drifting arches: and behind them all, unmoving, the true porch, square-cut, solid.

'The Mound must break! It cannot hide the door!'
'Yes,' said Roland. 'It's there. The door. It's real.'
'Then look! Now!'
Roland opened his eyes, and he saw the frame of the porch stamped in the turf, ghostly on the black hill. And as he looked the frame quivered, and without really changing, became another door; pale as moonlight, grey as ashwood; low; a square, stone dolmen arch made of three slabs – two uprights and a lintel. Below it was a step carved with spiral patterns that seemed to revolve without moving. Light spread from the doorway to Roland's feet.
'The door will be open as long as you hold it in your memory,' said Malebron.

From *Elidor*, Alan Garner

The blank piece of paper is a particularly intimidating threshold. Many of the exercises in this book are a means of enabling children to think about and articulate the process by which the writing is released from memory into words on the page. It is, of course, within the concrete imagery of story that children are most easily inducted into such abstract notions. There is, for instance, this moment in Alan Garner's *Elidor* when a threshold is crossed, a door opened. And the crossing is effected only through the power and intensity of Roland's thought. Only when he withdraws into a silence which is wholly active and creative, does the magic work. In this extract from the Chapter "The Mound of Vandwy", Roland must enter the Mound. There is no door and he must make one. Only through an intense act of memory can he recreate the door he knows best. Then that most ordinary door will become a magical threshold which he must cross to gain access to his heart's desire. This is, for the moment, quite simply, reunion with his family. So often magic lies within the commonplace relationships, encounters of our seemingly most ordinary lives. It is the peculiar power of story and poetry to enhance and transform all this ordinariness. Then memory evokes a nostalgia which leads to a recognition of the true heart's desire. And, like Roland, we are transported into another dimension. Here, for instance, Roland's concentration is so intense as he remembers the door in the house his family have just vacated that he sees:

'the blisters in the paint, and the brass flap with "Letters" outlined with dry metal polish."

This is so vivid that Roland believes the door is made, the crossing about to be effected. But it is not enough. He must withdraw again, painfully, into the deepest recesses of memory until, at last, the true porch emerges: "square-cut, solid." And then Roland knows. He is confident that the "true porch" is there. This is the measure of the commitment, the level of withdrawal into silence that children must experience in the classroom if they are to succeed as writers. It is most surely when they engage with stories like *Elidor* that the silence is not merely acceptable – it is seductive. This is all part of that vital collusion between teacher and storyteller. Within our literary heritage there are so many magical thresholds, no man's lands, places which are neither here nor there. And always there is the magical imperative that the barrier must be breached, the door opened. This is the impetus to write which will equip children with the will to withdraw, reflect upon and transform the ordinariness of their limited experience through the power of their words.

At this point a reading of Miroslav Holub's "The Door" reinforces the urgency of the crossing.

The Door

Go and open the door.
Maybe outside there's
a tree, or a wood,
a garden,
or a magic city.

Go and open the door.
Maybe a dog's rummaging.
Maybe you'll see a face,
or an eye,
or the picture
                of a picture.

Go and open the door.
If there's a fog
it will clear.

Go and open the door.
Even if there's only
the darkness ticking,
even if there's only
the hollow wind,
even if
        nothing
                is there,
go and open the door.

At least
there'll be
a draught.

Miroslav Holub

Surely those concluding lines are unarguable. But acknowledgement is as important as motivation if children are to develop confidence in their own experience as the basis of their imaginative writing. There must be moments which are social, convivial, in which the personal is shared and endorsed by the group. The compiling of a list of thresholds can be such a whole class activity. The final list may look something like this:

over the bridge	through the gate
across the ford	under the hedge
through the door	over the fence
behind the scenes	over the stepping stones
over the stile	across the ditch
round the corner	up the tree
down the stairs	through the window

(The importance of little words like prepositions is a by-product of the exercise.)

When children choose their theme, they write with the idea that the poem is a password. They will effect the crossing only if the words are right. These words must have all the power of the ancient and magical Open Sesame if they are to open the door to the enchanted place on the other side. Enchanted though this place may be, its magic depends on words which are unequivocally robust and most down to earth. It is, for instance, Clifford's uncompromising attention to concrete detail that takes us safely through the ford.

The Ford

I trot to the ford
On my pony,
Holding my breath
Because I know what happens.
He sees the talking, whispering water
And stops dead,
His legs stiff,
As if holding a heavy weight.
Then, he veers to the left,
His every muscle straining mine,
His hooves chatter on the road,
He rears like a flame,
And lands like spilt water.
Then, upset and shaking,
His feet touch the water,
His legs vibrating like a rubber band.

His neck is tense
And hard, tautly strung.
He leaps,
As if jumping from rooftop to rooftop,
And lands,
And trots shakily on.

Clifford Black, 12 years

Following this exercise the notion of 'threshold' can inform future writing on a variety
of themes and broaden out into issues of birth, death, initiation, and so much more.

I have found *Eden: Graphics and Poems* by Charles Tomlinson a rich source of
material. In particular, his poem "To be Engraved on the Skull of a Cormorant"
extends the threshold idea into issues of the transitoriness of life revealed in the residues
of beaks, skulls, feathers that line the threshold between life and death in our fields and
hedgerows.

To Be Engraved on the Skull of a Cormorant

across the thin
facade, the galleried-
with-membrane head:
narrowing, to take
the eye-dividing
declivity where
the beginning beak
prepares for flight
in a still-
perfect salience:
here, your glass
needs must stay
steady and your gross
needle re-tip
itself with reticence
but be
as searching as the sea
that picked and pared
this head yet spared
its frail acuity.

Charles Tomlinson

But this is a painter/poet and another dimension is available and caught in lines from his essay "The Poet as Painter":

"However much it (a skull) possesses of bleak finality, it also involves one in the fascination of inside and outside, that primary lure of the human mind seeking to go beyond itself ... and both anxious and enriched because of the sense of what lies behind or beneath those surfaces."

Then there is his "poem in prose": "Skullshapes" in which the poet/painter looks with that peculiar intensity which must precede the making. It is the painter speaking when he says:

"The skull of nature is recess and volume. The skull of art – of possibility – is recess, volume and also lines – lines of containment, lines of extension."

But this is also the vision of the poet, the paradoxical collusion between 'containment' and 'extension' which aspires to connect the particular with the universal. And, above all, it is this rich sense of 'possibility' which is the driving impetus to write and impels the writer to resolve his world in words, as surely as the artist must resolve it in lines. Here, Charles Tomlinson, artist/poet says:

"A cow skull opens a visionary field, a play of universals."

Kit's poem "Sheep's Skull", however halting, must have the audacity to aspire to this same vision.

Sheep's Skull

Wool,
Left over, like the silver trail of a snail . . .
On the ground
By the rusty barbed wire fence,
Where the rib cage rests on the tree trunk,
Like a broken bird cage,
Partly covered by a carcass.
The skull is . . .

A little doll's house.
And the eyes are filled with a light

That has filtered
Through the cascades of bone.
The teeth sit in their sockets,
Rattling,
Like a grandfather in a rocking chair.
They belong to a heavy smoker,
Black at the core and bottom.

At the back,
Vertebrae are attached,
Partly covered by the grass.

But now it's in the garden shed.
With a stick
Where the vertebrae once grew.
A cobweb across its eyes,
Blind to the outside world.

Kit Swindale 12, years

Seamus Heaney's "The Grauballe Man" is another poem which usefully extends the 'threshold' idea. Again, the poet looks with such intensity that his imagery tells a story, horrifying, and yet at the same time resonant with those echoes of our own histories in which we find our present.

The Grauballe Man

As if he had been poured
in tar, he lies
on a pillow of turf
and seems to weep

the black river of himself.
The grain of his wrists
is like bog oak,
the ball of his heel

like a basalt egg.
His instep has shrunk
cold as a swan's foot
or a wet swamp root.

His hips are the ridge
and purse of a mussel,
his spine an eel arrested
under a glisten of mud.

The head lifts,
the chin is a visor
raised above the vent
of his slashed throat

that has tanned and toughened.
The cured wound
opens inwards to a dark
elderberry place.

Who will say 'corpse'
to his vivid cast?
Who will say 'body'
to his opaque repose?

And his rusted hair,
a mat unlikely
as a foetus's.
I first saw his twisted face

in a photograph,
a head and shoulder
out of the peat,
bruised like a forceps baby,

but now he lies
perfected in my memory,
down to the red horn
of his nails,

hung in the scales
with beauty and atrocity:
with the Dying Gaul
too strictly compassed

on his shield,
with the actual weight
of each hooded victim,
slashed and dumped.

In the following two poems, first, Paul's enigmatic ending asserts our compulsion to connect with our past, to "dig again", no matter that inevitably "the thread snaps". Then there is Marilyn's visit to a museum, brought into new and vivid focus through her reading of "The Grauballe Man". The playfulness of her ending seems strangely fitting in this poem in which our present impinges on great issues of death and time. Always models must open up possibilities, never prescribe or constrain.

The Marsh Man

He lay under the bed of reeds
at Oak Field Marsh,
protected by peat.

Until one day an archaeologist,
who was digging for bones,
stumbled across this human dinosaur,

held together by the thinnest of threads.
Like the shadows of two
skyscrapers

touching tips together
but never colliding.

Oh no, never colliding
until the thread snaps
and then he's truly
dead in our minds.
Forever.
Until one day,
we dig again.

Paul Batley, 13 years

Dear Mummy

She lay
In her elaborate coffin
At the Hancock Museum.

I hated to see her . . .
Me staring at her.
And she, staring back
Through blind eyes.

Her face was brown and shrivelled,
Like an over-ripe potato
On the verge of mould.
Her mouth was screwed up,
Lips tightly pressed together
As though she had just bitten
Into the bitterest lemon.

Her hair, black as jet.
I was amazed she still had hair!
It looked coarse, dry.
I imagined it felt
Like wisps of steel wool.

Her nails were embedded
Into her rusty fingers.
Her skin was brown
And tarnished,
Like old shoe leather,
Sticking to her ribs.
Arms and legs were withered,
Like dying bean stalks.

When you die, you escape time.
But,
Here she is, still a prisoner,
Her body still confined
To Earth.

They say they're going to build up her face,
See what she really looked like.
Maybe she was an Egyptian Queen,
Cleopatra,
Nefertiti.
Maybe she will look like me!

But hasn't she aged well!

Marilyn Rust, 13 years

Time

My Grandma lived in a basement flat.
I imagined it as an underground hole.
And my Grandma, a creature, hiding scared
From the outside world.
Caught in time.
The staircase bent around
Like a huge Chinese Dragon
With a million bright colours
In the carpet.
The carpet itself was shaggy and heavy . . .

A big, hairy dog could easily get lost in it,
Or so I thought.
From the window two rectangles of light
Melted onto the carpet.
The dust flew,
Caught in those two rays of light,
Caught like Grandma,
Caught in time.
And if I, too, stepped into those rectangles,
Would I be caught forever, like dust?
Would I be caught like Grandma?
For the very last time.

Joanne Ireland, 13 years

Starling

A jeweller's skilled hands shaped a small jet stone
That was born an eye.
An eye that now stares, so terror-stricken.
The eye is looking out from a starling's torn feather coat.
The broken china bird limps across the arm of the chair.
And flaps his stiff wings in a last attempt to escape.
He lands.
A dead heap on the floor.
Lost the battle with the closed windows,
And now is battered and bent.
A young bird and yet so old and crooked.

The jet stone eye, so beautifully crafted by the jeweller,
Still stares.

Helen Walkey, 13 years

The Time of Day

A tiny, near-bald rat,
Out of a sun-coloured mother.
He grew, suckling milk as warm and rich
As compost.
A knock-kneed puppy,
One ear tumbled over his eye,
Like a stubborn forelock.
His fur was imitation gold velvet,
The gold at the fringe
Of a fresh sun-risen autumn stream.
It is morning.

He has grown,
His legs have straightened,
His coat has mellowed,
His muscles ripple as water-filled balloons
As he leaps, the blue and green ball
Caught.
In memory
As he comes to earth
The sun has climbed; it is noon.

He will tire,
The balloons will burst,
And the water drain away.
The blue and green ball
Will wear thin, and rot from damp.
The light from his sun-coloured mother
Will have been extinguished long ago.
He will lie in front of a new fire,
Lapping cold, treated milk,
As hollow to taste
As licking Christmas envelopes for the world.
And his coat will lose its shine,
Grow unfocused,
The halo of a summer sunset
In the late evening.

And his face will wrinkle,
His sight will blur,
Eyes trying to look through seawater.
The newborn kitten,
Trying vainly to pump blood through his ancient body

Will give up, tired of work,
And he will die.
For the Sun-dog's coat will shine no more;
For one day all stars will die,
And there will be eternal night.

Stephen Gardam, 13 years

10 Dreams and Hauntings

I have already described how Ted Hughes's dream sequence fable *What Is The Truth?* can work in the classroom. Lately, however, it has been the dream element which has provided new perspectives. God leads the Son down to earth at night because this is when men sleep. He explains:

> "In their sleep, they will say what they truly know. That is another odd thing about mankind. When they are awake, they are deepest asleep. When they are asleep, they are widest awake. Strange creatures!"

Awake, we are besieged by all the distractions of the outside world, our fickle attention so easily broken by the clamour of our busy lives. It is in our dreams we come closest to that state of introspective awareness that is the mark of the poet. Moreover, in all the kaleidoscopic, shifting images of the dream state the unconscious mind sifts the memories, perceptions and impressions of the waking life to create a bizarre, surreal world which has its own peculiar truth. Tom Stacey, writing about the requirement for narrative in his article "The Special Pact", says,

> "The function of the dream demonstrates man's extraordinary will for metaphor and narrative. Dogs dream, but man being distinguished from the beast by consciousness, the word must go on from the dream and give the wakened mind its narratives."

In *What Is The Truth* for instance, there is a dreaming dog but it is the farmer who is endowed with the word and must go on to speak the poem:

> I was carrying our cat.
> Across a ploughed field. Above us, a blue-black piled-up sky
> Boiled bulgy clouds.
> I thought: it's like giant blackberries. And I thought:
> If it rains, I'll be a queer colour.
>
> There came a crack of lightning.
> It was like being cracked over the skull with a splintering bamboo.
> The lid flew off everything. I saw the blue-hot centre.

I thought: This is it, a planet's crashed into us.
And our cat was so scared, it peed all warm down my shirt.

Then everything was alright again.
Except our cat had turned into some kind of bird
That started struggling to fly. I had to hold it hard.
The thing about this bird
Was it was made of gold.

All soft warm scale-armour, its feathers were scales
And every scale was the flame of a candle
Hammered out flat – part solid, but the gold fringe still soft flame,
And I knew these flames were off candles
That angels had held. Suddenly this bird
Burst free and bounced onto the tilth in front of me
And stood there, dishevelled.
Then it shook its flames into shape, it whirled itself
Like a bottleful of bright coins, and stood brighter.
It had horns on its head. And I saw its head

Was a word in Chinese.
I stared into its flame, I couldn't stare into it hard enough.
And I stared at its head –
I knew that word had a meaning
But the meaning was too big, I had to hold my head in
Because I could feel it trying to split.
It was a funny dream all right.
Then my head actually split – the two halves came right apart
And the bird was looking at me, I saw its barbed tongue
And it let out a yell, and I woke up –

What I'd heard was a pheasant.

Ted Hughes

Similarly, when children attempt a dream sequence poem, they receive a licence to coin bizarre, surreal imagery, to allow weird, almost arbitrary metamorphoses which assert connections unthinkable in the wakened state. And because a poem is crafted and conscious, it imparts a coherence to those images. This coherence, as it emerges from the pattern of the poem, makes a robust kind of sense which restores us to this earth, awake, renewed and aware. This is even more assured when children write within rôle. As they enter the dream of the blacksmith, the farmer, the fisherman, they gain access to a store of impressions, memories, sensations they did not realise they possessed. Just as in the

Christmas exercise, "The Witnesses", the rôles must be stereotypes in order to assert the universality within which we will make our individual and unique connections. And as these unstructured, shifting dreams submit to the unifying craft of the poet, all sorts of unconscious allusions float up to the surface of the mind to be caught in the pattern of the poem. Surely, for instance, there are lingering memories of *Alice in Wonderland* when Timothy finds himself diminishing into:

> "a forty year old grain of dust"

and the chickens become:

> "giant sewing machines
> Dipping their over-sized needles."

Children can write only within the firmly established patterns of their literary heritage whose forms and symbols must constantly emerge and recur within their own developing writing.

The Farmer's Nightmare

> The farmer slept . . .
> And dreamed . . .
> He was feeding the chickens in the rain,
> Clutching onto his battered bucket of feed,
> Swaying from side to side,
> In the gale force wind.
> He found himself mingling with the sand on the floor,
> Like a forty year old grain of dust.
> The chickens pecked around him,
> Like giant sewing machines,
> Dipping their over-sized needles
> All about his tiny body.
> Then he found himself tall again,
> Looking down on his chickens,
> As they huddled in twos.
> Crushed up.
> The feathers joined,
> And ironed out into golden petals.
> Their scrawny legs connected.
> And gradually changed colour and texture,
> To turn into stems.
> Then, the wings turned into the leaves
> Of a buttercup . . . floating,
> Protected from the wind by the chicken huts.
> Then the farmer awoke.
> And cringed at the light of day.

> *Timothy Overton, 12 years*

So often there are tiny details which, in all the heat and fury of the headlong progress of the dream, provide a tenuous but crucial hold on the reality to which the poem is committed to return us. For instance, in the following example it is most surely as the midnight thunderstorm breaks and:

> "Gran's old tablecloth
> flapped in the gale as rain started to pour –
> she'd left it out all night."

that we begin to know ploughing and harvest in the poetic sense. And that is to know it most really.

A Ploughing Dream

At midnight – still.
The old plough turfed up clumps of wet mud.
A slash with a whip
and a kick up the ass.
"Goa on!"
roared the farmer.
A great crack in the purple sky
opened daylight for a split second.
Gran's old tablecloth
flapped in the gale as rain started to pour –
she'd left it out all night.
The leather strap unreeled
to slash its guts
to bloody ribbons, slithering to a bucket of eels.
The horse pulled away –
snapped the straps,
heeled on its hind legs
and stumped the cart with its front teeth –
the size of building bricks.
Storming off into the darkness,
only two massive haunches showing,
like loose muscles dancing.

The farmer
stumbled to the ground
and started to pull –
heaving –
slipping his feet
in the mud.
The thunder roared
and the sky reopened,

leaving a maroon mist.
His muscles snapping
and breaking all over,
getting nowhere.
The plough no longer ploughing,
he fell to the mud,
studding his back –
slapping his arms down to the puddles,
tying his wrists down with his whip.
He gave up,
naked.

Robert Filby, 12 years

Deborah writes as a blacksmith and again the distancing effect of rôle and dream returns her so vividly to her own experiences of horses, stables and forges:

A Blacksmith's Dream

The golden geese . . .
come to have their feet manicured.
Harps are sewn into their feet.
The harps sizzle,
and the geese lash out,
beating and hitting the coal miner.
The miner gets to work on his tune,
hitting nails and clashing tools.
He makes his band.
Then the bird,
head low and wings spread,
flees for his life.
The forge,
like the sky,
throws out stars.
Along comes another goose,
wanting lameness cured.
But with all his tunes and stars gone,
The coal miner packs up.
Then one last star burns him.
And he wakes . . .
and the only reminder,
a small brown burn on his arm.

Deborah Swain, 13 years

Clare recounts the dream of the fisherman. Here again, the imagery is vivid, uncompromising, and yet committed utterly to reality. There is, for instance, just as "The stars teetered and fell", the creative use of cliché in: "God boomed blue murder". This has the peculiar and reassuring effect of reminding us of our everyday world in which disaster can be swaddled so cosily in meaningless phrases. By the end of this poem, however, that complacency is destroyed in a re-discovery of the elemental forces which hover on the very fringes of our comfortable lives.

The Fisherman's Dream

On the black horizon
A bullet-bodied whale
Writhed like a flame
In the purple sea.
A three-headed gull
Sat on the old man's shoulder,
As ribbons of light
Whipped the evil sky, brutally,
Cracking it apart.
The stars teetered and fell,
And God boomed blue murder
As he repaired his cracked floor.
The whale had arrived.
The sea glared red-violet
As the whale swelled
And the fisherman plunged a harpoon
Deep through the lycra-tight skin . . .
Muddy blood gurgled through the blubber.
It reminded him of the last time he scraped his boots.
It dissolved the falling stars,
And melted the whale's flesh.
Another silver snake
Sliced the angered sky.
The lighthouse moon teetered,
Then fell.
The roaring lion-whale died,
Sizzling in its blood.
Limp in the water.
The old fisherman stared . . .
And the falling stars
Burnt his paling skin.
He woke.
And the hot cigarette fell from his face.

Clare Watkinson, 12 years

The Myth and the Dream

In his essay, "Myth and Education", Ted Hughes says of the Greek myths:

" . . . those supernatural, seeming dreams were projections of man's inner and outer world.
Any fragment of the story serves as the 'word' by which the whole story's electrical circuit is switched into consciousness, and all its light and power brought to bear."

The Persephone myth is such a story. It serves as the 'word' with all the power to restore us to the earth and satisfy those atavistic impulses which are so easily alienated within our consumer society. Most especially, this is one of those stories which we feel we have always known. During a re-telling in the classroom there is a dawning sense of recognition and pleasure which is the mark of a shared endeavour to make sense of the world. This is a moment of listening which is so essentially social that it is almost collaborative. Above all, there is all the warmth of a tribal celebration of wisdom on a chosen common ground. And yet this is a story about alienation, withdrawal, and it is within this particular context that the individual is empowered to withdraw and reflect. Just as Persephone, exiled in the cold bleakness of the underworld, reflects with nostalgia on the fruitful earth which is her home, so we are endowed with a new and startling perspective on all that we have so fatally taken for granted. This engagement between earth and underworld releases imagination and, at the same time, reconciles the private and public aspects of the writer's craft. Ted Hughes, again writing generally about the Greek myths, says:

"A story which engages . . . earth and the underworld . . . contains not merely the space . . . and the contents of those two places; it reconciles their contradictions in a workable fashion and holds open the way between them."

He continues that for the child this is "the beginning of a form of contemplation". To teach contemplation is the ultimate challenge for the teacher of English. It can be attempted only within our great tribal dreams. And only within such engagements are our dreams renewed within each generation and our health restored. Some exercises enable children to dream within a dream. For instance, the following exercise links the old story to present reality. At the same time it distances the writer from the commonplace of his own life in order that he might rediscover it:

Imagine Persephone trapped in the cold darkness of the underworld. Homesick, she dreams of the fruitful earth she has left behind.

The following two poems are responses to this exercise.

The Dream of Persephone

Persephone dreams . . .
Of sun streaming
Like her favourite yellow ribbon . . .
And the dot to dot stars
Drawing the sky . . .
The rock pool
With flowing hair
Held by clips of eels,
Cousins of worms
Who feed the mole
With his soft silk coat,
Black, that contrasts the wings
Of the cabbage whites,
Fluttering
Like the flames of candles.
She watches the sunset fade
And the dot to dot
Stars are drawing the sky.
Then, her yellow ribbon,
Her favourite,
Looks like sun-streaming
Dreams.

Phoebe Wingate, 11 years

The Dream of Persephone

Persephone dreams,
Dreams of a meadow
Where nothing is still,
Nothing is sad or lonely.
A giant multi-coloured spotted quilt –
A patch of picture-book poppies
Sways in the wind.
A stronger breeze blows them
And their petals
Turn into thousands of red butterflies.
A cloud forms,
Blotting out the sun,
Leaving a red light.
But soon it scatters
And just long grasses remain.
Slug trails cover a large stone

Like a child's first drawing.
The trees lining the meadow
Have crows' nests on their tops,
Hair with specks of dirt.
And an apple tree grows ping-pong ball fruit.
A brook runs through this paradise
Like a silver ribbon
Binding it up into reality.

Jane Weaver, 12 years

For those children who want to make a more topical response to the old story there is the option of a myth for our own time:

> Imagine an astronaut exiled in the clinical austerity of his space craft. His senses crave the good earth which is his home. Write a poem in which the earthsick astronaut dreams.

This time the physical distancing of the space craft returns children to their familiar farms, fields and hedgerows with a nostalgic sense of discovery and urgency.

Memories From Space

I miss the Earth from up here.
Now I see it as a roller
Used for printing patches on newly born cows.
I remember walking through the fields
In which they grazed . . .
The smell of dung, earth, dead leaves and twigs
Was a smell sweeter than honey.
Now missed but before unnoticed.
The leaves, fossilised trees,
And me fossilised within my
        Memories.

Marie Fenn, 13 years

Astronaut

He stood, gazing at the earth, dreaming of his flower garden . . .

Green tips of seedlings poking from the compost,
opening their leaves to be warmed by the Sun,
the Sun bouncing off the greenhouse:
tomatoes turned orange to red

and worms crawled in the damp soil, sunning their skins.
His wife planted seedlings; making a hole with her index finger,
she eased in the marigold.
He missed catching the 7.56 to Leeds,
the click of the typewriter printing a's and e's
on the headed note-paper.
He missed the tone of the telephone
and the lift saying "Going up".
Then there were . . .

Sunny afternoons on the heath,
wandering down sheep paths,
in amongst the heather.
Heather, a blaze of colour like fire,
reds and oranges.
And when he got home there would be
crumpets rich with butter,
crumpets like the moon . . .

Like the moon.

Sara Worts, 12 years

The Earthsick Astronaut

He is yearning for his earth senses.
He wants the smell of burning wood to swirl up
And tickle his nose
Like a coarse, rough feather from a bird on the earth;
He wants the sight of a fire,
The flickering fish tails
That make his eyes see nothing else;
He wants to taste bacon, the real bacon,
Tingling on his tongue to evoke
The smell, the sound, the flavour . . .
He wants the touch of cold air on his skin;
Air, a free spirit, teasing, running;
A brush-past kiss on a warm cheek is
His memory;
And then . . . the sad things;
Gravestones like babies' teeth, yet
Decayed with lichen and moss.
But still he is yearning,
Yearning for air, for fire,
For Earth.

Leanora Dack, 12 years

Hauntings

The great tradition of ghost stories is always a favourite with children. They relish the hooting owls in moonlit churchyards, the rattling chains, the disembodied voices. Unhappily, these clichés transfer only too readily into their own writing. Ghosts are dangerous. They are so bound by cliché they may dull the vision, provide a soft option of jaded phrases. Leon Garfield's short story "A Grave Misunderstanding" is, however, just the kind of story to exorcise the over-familiar. It is set in a graveyard and has all the ingredients of the predictable. But this is a master storyteller and he creates a ghost who is the very essence of the place, an elusive concentration of earthy autumn air, leaf mould and pine. This is a ghost whose very presence sharpens perceptions and provides a different perspective on all those haunted churchyards. Only the dog is aware that this is a ghost and as he barks desperate warnings to his hopelessly infatuated master, we deplore the blunt senses of human-beings. Now we know we are ill-equipped to live either safely or happily on this earth we call our home. This ghost is the basis of the children's poems. She is dynamic, with at least the latent power of a catalyst on her surroundings. And, most importantly, her claim is on the senses. She is real. She *is* the place. As the children write their poems, their senses must be as sharply attuned to their chosen place as the dog's were to the churchyard. Only then will they see their ghost.

Ghost of the Sea

Ancient fingers
Search for you
Through to your soul,
Shiver down your spine as if her hand is on your back.
Her finger-nails of fish scales . . .
And she is biting your mind.
Mist is reaching to your heart
When it crawls over the frantic waves.
The waves foam,
The strands of her past life.
The cliffs crumble like her chalk teeth
Where seaweed hangs.
Little shells carrying the water,
Climb to the beach
Like maidens of old time
Fetching water from the well.
Whistle in the wind and the ghost will appear.
Her face,
Lacy like fishing tackle,
Moulded from a gull's nest . . .
Feathers and cracked shell left behind in her dreamless mind.
Her silk cloak and cobwebs hang from her armpits;
Her bleached hair
And her wispy voice tell you . . .
"Never come again."

Robert Filby, 12 years

The Ghost of the Orchard

She walks through overgrown grass,
With apple silk feet.
Her face is round and sweet as an apple,
Yet tainted with the sourness
Of apples gone bad, dreams gone bad.
Crystallised thoughts, held still in an empty head,
With beads that rattle as she walks, talks.
Her breath is the mist on cold morning air,
As her dry silk ball gown, moth eaten, brushes past
Dead trees and wilting flowers.
She smells of old cider and mothballs
And apples in wicker baskets,
Tunnelled by wasps.
Her eyes are twirling apple pips.
Sad and forgotten.
She shakes her head and her coils of ebony hair,
Like blackberries, shake too,
Shaking out smells of smoky straw and rotten fruit.
Her voice is like a feather falling through the air . . .
"Who will dance with me?"

The wind shall dance with you, my dear,
Dance a cider waltz around your trees,
Through your veins and your hollow voice
The wind blows through and through . . .

"Who will dance . . . ?"

Emma Walkey, 12 years

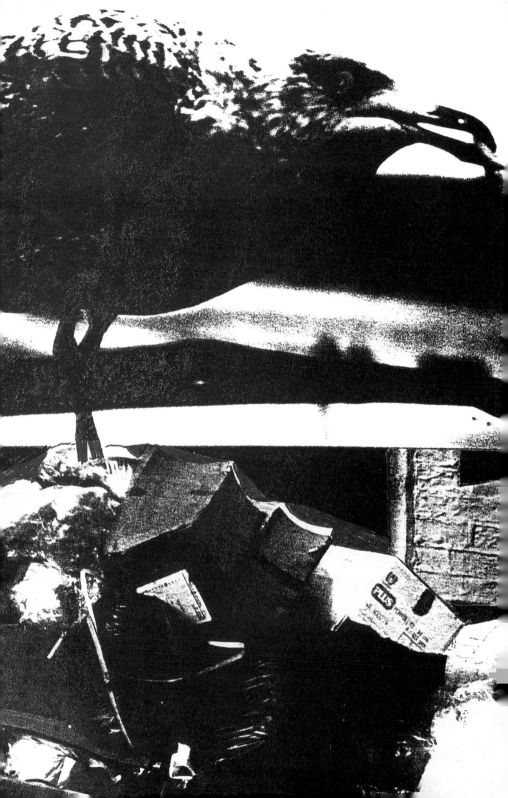

11 Poetry and the Environment

The environmental implications of the work in the poetry classroom have already been indicated. This chapter is an attempt to describe some of the ideas which impinge most directly on 'green' issues.

Children have a deep and intuitive sense of affinity with the environment. Their closeness with earth is expressed most readily and naturally when they scramble over rocks, plunge their hands into rock pools, climb trees, or fish with an extraordinarily intense concentration. All this, however, is usually spontaneous, unreflecting, and it is not until the quiet moment of withdrawal makes space for reflection, that these intuitive feelings can develop into a sense of respect and responsibility.

In *Poetry in the Making*, Ted Hughes says of beauty spots:

"These are the remains of what the world was once like all over. They carry us back to the surroundings our ancestors lived in for 150 million years – which is long enough to grow to feel quite at home even in a place as wild as the uncivilised earth."

When we visit a wild place we experience a sense of homecoming. We satisfy a hungry nostalgia we did not know we possessed. Again, Ted Hughes says that what makes landscapes valuable to us is

"not simply the presence of the elements, but the encounter between the elemental things and the living, preferably the human."

In the following poem, for instance, Matthew's perception of the old man's connection with the tree is, at once, a recognition of a common life source and a celebration of earth which amounts to a developing sense of responsibility. Moreover, the fallen rainforests are inextricably linked with Matthew's blasted tree. Poetry transcends space and time as surely as it transcends sentimentality. And not only does it extend horizons, it inculcates values more surely than any amount of didactic teaching.

The Tree and Uncle George

The tree stands,
Charred as a used match.
Lightning destroyed the mighty oak,
But still there stands a four foot stump
Fifteen years after its fiery fall.

The death of Uncle George
Is woven into the tree's departure.
The way he used to limp
Through Henham Woods
As the rain slowly seeped
Through his battered raincoat.
His half bald head
Covered in a film of water
That shimmered in the sun
Like an over-glazed pot.

At times the sun
Shone down on his wrinkled face,
Lighting the creases
Like furrows on a field.
And his worn shoes
were the cut-off roots of the stricken tree,
Wedging him firmly
To the living earth.

Matthew Booley, 13 years

But the problem is, of course, that those atavistic impulses which would return us to wilderness earth for the sustenance we crave are so intuitive that often they remain unrealised. The country children of Halesworth have all the detachment from the beauties of the Waveney Valley which precludes sentimentality. Moreover, it is this detachment which has all the potential for direct, robust writing. But they may all too readily take their surroundings so much for granted that they look without seeing, know without realising. There must be strategies which address this problem by providing different and unusual perspectives. In particular, I have found the Bible story of Bartimaeus the Blind Beggar an effective means of encouraging children to look as though for the first time ever. This is, of course, to look with the eye of the poet. Here is a man who had never seen. When he recovers his sight, the world is startling. His other senses, so sharply attuned over the sightless years, combine with his eyes to batter his perceptions with colour, shape, sound and texture. Always I hope that the story will be so well known to the children through all the rich cadences and rhythms of the Authorised Version that, again, it will be one of those stories that they feel they have always known, deeply and within their very bones. In order to give the story new immediacy and impact, I provide a re-telling:

Bartimaeus

I've been able to see for over a year now. But I'm still not used to it. In a way I'm glad that I was once blind because I'll never take my eyes for granted. I think I'll always look at the world as though I'm seeing it for the first time. You see, I'd been blind from birth. Yes, I was happy. I suppose you are if you don't realise what you are missing. I managed to get by with the help of neighbours and I wasn't above a spot of begging, especially where there were crowds and the promise of some good pickings.

Anyway, it was about a year ago that young David began to talk about a man who had come out of the desert. There was talk of miracles, healings, all sorts of wild rumours. Some even said he claimed to be the Son of God. Well, we're used to strange types round here. They come and go and I've never taken much notice. As I said, I'd learned to live with my blindness and I knew that there was no cure. David, however, thought that he knew better. This man from the desert (Jesus, he called him) had brought a dead girl back to life and David was sure he could do something for me. It seemed this Jesus was coming to town that afternoon and David would not be satisfied until I agreed to go out and try to meet him. At least there would be crowds and I could hope for a full begging bowl at the end of the day.

The trouble was the sun was hot, I developed a raging thirst and got almost trampled to death. I would never have stuck it out if David hadn't been with me. At last we heard shouting in the distance and the crowd surged forward. I sat there helpless until David suddenly tugged at my robe: "Go on, shout! He's passing by!" he yelled.

Well, I filled my lungs and roared. I hadn't waited there all day to miss my chance when it came. People standing round tried to shut me up but I could feel David dancing up and down beside me and joining his voice to mine. Then, suddenly, everything went quiet except for my own voice. I felt foolish, and sat there, very still. People began talking, quietly this time; hands lifted me to my feet. "This way; he wants to meet you," they murmured. Then I heard his voice: "Bartimaeus." Goodness knows how he knew my name. Anyway there was no point in beating about the bush. "I want my sight. Can you help me?" I asked. There was a short silence and I felt something wet and cold smeared on my eyelids. "Go and wash in the pool," said the voice.

I felt David's hand slipped into mine. It was trembling with excitement. And then he was pulling me, leading me to the water. The crowd dispersed to let us through and soon I felt the cool mud of the river seeping into my sandals. And then I was on my knees, my face in the water. I pressed my finger tips onto my closed eyelids and washed and washed. I raised my head and opened my eyes. I looked into a grey light. The grey broke into jigsaw patterns which danced and flickered before they swam slowly into focus. I don't quite know what I expected to see but I simply couldn't make sense of anything. I didn't realise I was looking into David's face until he spoke. "Can you see me?" he asked.

I jumped at the voice coming from the face. I thought I knew all about faces. I'd felt David's often enough; and yet I was unprepared for the reality. You see, I knew all about textures and shapes but I knew nothing about light and shade, colours. I didn't know life flickered out of eyes like that. I stared and stared and it was some time before anyone could get any sense out of me.

Well, I've been seeing for a year now. I'll never forget waking up that first morning in time to see my first sunrise. Funnily, all the sunrises since have seemed just as new. I can't understand why you people who have always been able to see won't use your eyes. That's why I'm almost glad I was blind for thirty years. Now I can see. And every day is a miracle.

And then, as the children take on the rôle of the blind beggar to write their own poems, the scales fall from their own eyes and they write about this earth with a sense of urgency and discovery hitherto unattainable. Most importantly, they exercise a sense of value.

Bartimaeus

I open my eyes.
The world is a tiny particle of sand,
Growing each day.
I see the tree,
The bark,
As rough as an old woman's hand,
But smooth as chalk rubbings,
Leaves, crisp,
So fragile,
As fragile as finely painted porcelain,
Crumbling at the slightest touch.

I thought I knew everything about earth.
But . . .
I didn't know that
Waves crashed together
Like two cymbals.
Or that . . .
Biting into a crisp apple
Was like stepping on dry bracken

I thought I knew everything about animals.
But . . .
What about cows?
Their mouths,
Saliva dripping
Like water running.
And their udders,
Unripe plums
Left in the sun too long.

I was in darkness.
Now I'm in light.
The real world,
Forever.

Nicola Steele, 13 years

The poetry children write within the context of *What Is The Truth?* frequently has 'green' implication. As they choose the creature they will attempt to 'name', many children consider endangered species. Although there is often a poignancy in their choice of rhino, gorilla, hare, whale etc., they understand that, within the context of this fable, it is the 'truth' of their chosen creature which must be addressed. If, like the wizards of Earthsea, they succeed in their 'naming', then the spell will be cast and not only will their creature emerge most surely from their words, it will assert its right to life. There will be no need to preach a message. In the following poem, for instance, it is as Joanna describes the birth of piglets that modern farming methods become the hidden focus.

The Maternity Ward

Number 124,
Born 10,
Dead 2.
The maternity ward,
Dung hissing, the bloodstained floor, the piglets inside skin,
The sow lies,
In her cot of metal bars,
Rolls of fat, tidal waves,
Underneath no room for expansion.
A piglet stands in her tiny stiletto shoes,
Her heel stuck through the orange plastic floor,
A sieve for muck and membrane.
Her mother gently woos her
With soft grunts of wisdom.
The piglet totters for her first found food

to find the wonder of outside and inside combined.
The pig's soft skin, gently woven by nature
Into a spider web fleece.
Her skin, the colour of heaven on a sunny day.
A new beginning
Ending for the day to come.
A whirl of blood.
No more.
And the piglet sucks on.

Joanna Tyler, 13 years

Similarly, Paul mourns the decreasing herds of Highland ox. On holiday in Scotland, he feels first a sense of permanency, caught so movingly in his Biblical allusion, and then, a sense of devastating loss.

Highland Ox

I once knew a beast that roamed
In the Highlands;
Its horns were a truncheon,
Big,
Battered.
The matted hair was an orangoutang's chest,
Or a half dried wig
Tossed and strewn about.
Its legs were oak stumps,
The rings showing age,
With a dry crust of mud for bark,
Flaky,
Crumbled.
It had the skin of a rhino
And was tough as leather.
It was wild,
Could have known John the Baptist,
The locusts and honey.
He wandered all day,
But never moved,
Chewing the same cud for years,
Worn white.
Until, one day,
Some men parked a landrover on the brow of a hill.
One wielded a shot gun.
Suddenly, a crack!

Doves shot out of a nearby forest;
A dog whimpered half a mile away.
And there was a thud
Of rock,
Clay
And heaving bones.
I never saw him again.

Paul Sparkes, 13 years

Then there is Emma who, in naming her elephant, attempts almost incidentally to express a wistful sense of its vulnerability.

The Last Elephant

The Elephant came furthest of all.
He followed the star.
His legs carried his weight for so long
his socks fell down
and made life-long wrinkles.
His ears, ragged,
like a well-worn scarf,
his eyes, brown painted rocks,
smoothed off and gentle
to form great pearls of wisdom,
leading the way across the plains.
His body was as if
he was the most comfortable of all
in his baggy clothing.
His wrinkles were like the ones in the sand,
delicate and always there.

Emma Neilson, 13 years

The Barn Owl

The Barn Owl is the Duchess of the woods.
She lifts her wings
As if hitching her skirt to her knees.
Her silk bloomer legs throw her into the air,
And then comes her magical flight. . . .
Her wings beat with grace – and power.
Then . . .
She glides through the air.
Her X-ray vision scans the ground beneath.

You or I would say that that was just a pebble.
But the owl knows that that pebble is a mouse.
The mouse knows that the Duchess wants her rent,
But, of course, he cannot pay.
So she takes his life.

She stops,
Hovers,
Dives,
And lands on the pebble exactly.
Her cat-like talons pierce the mouse's skin
And now the mouse has paid with his life.

William Mair, 10 years

Whale   I uncurl the sea,
And you're there.
Staring with giant oyster eyes
Set in deep curves of muscle.
Your streamlined back,
Like black silk over hot wax.

Barnacles cling to your skin
Like limpet mines to an old ship.
Your giant mouth opens,
Releasing an eerie wailing cry . . .
Your air vent,
Shaped like a milk bottle nozzle,
Opens and lets out hot air,
Creating a spout of steam.

Surely you must be admired
For your knowledge.
But you are better known for meat,
Or fat.

You bear a scar to prove it,
A deep gash in your side,
Cut like a slice of water melon.
The spear fell out long ago
And now you are dying.

The last whale floats to the surface,
Like a great island.

Gavin Thurlow, 13 years

A Shrew

A shrew
is fierce.
A versatile sort of chap
with a long pointed nose,
like a pen nib with a black pimple on the end,
which sniffs its way through pebbles, stones or wire netting –
or give each obstacle a nudge in a temper.
Its long brows hang over its eyes with a sharp look.
It's like water trickling over pebbles in a stream
as it scurries about.
Just bones,
with a short covering of fur and a long pink tail.
The trap goes.
This shrew was fierce.

Robert Filby, 10 years

Gorilla – Mother of Earth

There she sat,
Slumped against the wall of her enclosure,
Like a sack of soot.
A lonely figure.

Her sad eyes,
The colour of damp soil,
Played at my conscience,
Begging to be free.

Her skin was the colour
Of a midnight pond,
Shiny and black.
A deep, set frown
Was embedded into her forehead,
Rivers of worry.

Her hair was black.
Black as the world!
Each hair stood out,
Magnifying her solitary presence.

Hands dipped in coal dust
Gripped tightly onto a doll.
Once there had been a baby.
Finger nails, dark brown,
Needed a manicure.

And there she was.
Mother Earth
In person.
An outcast
Of a greedy world!

Marilyn Rust, 13 years

Hare

His nose twitches,
three tiny olives in the shape of a pie chart.
He smells the strong scent
of Wild Mushrooms.
Before he was born his world was black,
black as the wayward sheep.
Nothing to smell or see.
Now he is overwhelmed.
Now, for the first time, his heart
clashes with his mother's.
His coat, matted with membrane,
dries, crisp in the sun,
like a dog's fresh from a swim.

Through spring he grows,
his coat glows gold.
His ears stand firm,
like two heads from wooden spoons.
His eyes focus in the light
and from them shines his youth.
The muscles in his legs strengthen
and his speed, like his mother's,
is miraculous.

As he runs, there is a click in the undergrowth,
a second to aim, then . . .
Crack!
A shot like a dropping pan
fills the clearing.

An ear-splitting cry,
like the highest note
on the most out of tune violin . . .

The hare falls.
Dying, he returns to the darkness.

William Mair, 12 years

The Rhino

The rhino is a child's model
made out of clay,
the crinkly folds casting shadows
over its rainy day back.
Its big sad eyes stare at you
as if to say, "Help me."
His creased eyelids blink
back the tears.

His legs – stubbed out cigarette ends,
Wallow in the mud, making craters
in the soil.
The horn – a huge cornet
of matted hair –
is the jinx of the rhino.
That is all he is hunted for.
And the lead from the bullets
has turned his skin grey.

Kirsty Butcher, 13 years

Finally, Leanora, again writing with the context of *What Is The Truth?* draws inspiration
from the story of St Francis. She has the sure knowledge that if the creature is 'named'
accurately in metaphor then it will answer the call. And there is all the power of the
poet's enchantment as she writes within the rôle of the saint.

The Call of St Francis

Come to me –
And bring me your truths.

Fish,
Swim to me;
Let your fins

Like softened sea shells
Hear my call and bring
A lock of my hair,
Turned green by algae,
Sealed in your memory
Of plants and stones,
Forward to the sea of my making.

Bird,
Fly to me;
Let your wings
Feel my call and bring
The snap of your beak,
As sharp as the sound that you heard
When you broke into my world,
Forward to the tree of my making.

Animal,
Run to me.
Rabbit,
Let the spring uncoil and
Leap to me
With bent-back ears
Like ballerina's feet.

Snake,
Crawl to me
On your chess-board stomach
and tell me the secrets of the ground.
Lion,
Run to me
With your mane of arrogance
And paws like clover leaves
And share your jungle with me.
Hear my call and bring to me
The space of your desert
Like the palm of my hand;
My sweat,
Your feverish heat.

Walk by my side
Or fly at my shoulder;
Swim at my feet
And give me your souls;
Make me whole with your stories of life
And make yourselves whole with mine.

Leanora Dack, 13 years

Frequently, natural forces pose a threat to the environment and then there are strong accompanying feelings of fear and helplessness. Dunwich, a small Suffolk coastal village was once a thriving city comprising nine parish churches and a busy harbour. Over the centuries the sea has eaten at the coastline until today all that remains is a small village and one last gravestone from the last church, All Saints.

In the recent gales which have swept the shores, erosion has been accelerated and man's culpability in the changing climatic conditions is, at least, a matter for conjecture. Here, Stephen contemplates the awesomeness of nature and expresses the fearfulness which is so often a necessary prerequisite to that acceptance and respect which is finally resolved only in a sense of responsibility.

Dunwich

On the corner, there is a walnut tree.
Stretching its gnarled limbs
High,
For the wind to turn its leaves
To face the sea.
To face the sea that didn't used to be;
When the walnut tree had no reason to stretch before the wind.

Now a car park, one or two tufts of rope blowing,
Commands the bottom of the picture;
A picture unframed; wild but tamed.
The new café to the right,
Marshy dunes to the left.
But, at the top,
The sea, the sky,
The fishing boats.
Carved, wood splintering,
Lying like a herd of well-fed
But hollow sea-cows.
Then the sea.

Grey, tops of the waves just brushed with white,
With the farthest curve of the stony beach
Stuck niggling in one corner
With the crumbling cliffs
A line of formless village elders;
Elders of the village of Britain
Sat in a never-ending war council against the sea.

And losing the cold war.

Stephen Gardam, 13 years

It is most surely within the poetry classroom that children's feelings about their environment are given the status of objective expression. Only as they read and write within a literary context can they transform the facts through the power of metaphor and achieve an uncompromising language which transcends easy sentimentality. Strangely, it is even as feeling is stirred and the poem is written that a child confronts reality. And this is the basis of environmental education. It is also the beginning of hope for Planet Earth.

12 The Common Ground

Poetry is in no way élitist. I find more and more that it has as much to offer the less able child as his more able contemporary and can properly form the basis of his language work. The common humanity we share implies a common wavelength of literacy and we should not make the kind of concessions to the less able which exclude them from this wavelength. They must be freed to write well at the level of which they are capable. To achieve this we must dare to apply the same underlying principles; many less able children have a natural affinity with poetry and thus respond well to these. They experience the relief that few words are required, and the security provided by pattern and structure. When listening to poetry they have a deep and natural pleasure in rhyme and rhythm. Moreover, in their writing there is often a refreshing directness and simplicity of expression which a more intelligent child has to struggle to achieve. Often this more 'literary' child's verbal dexterity and more extensive vocabulary create problems of wordiness, turgidity, and metaphors which are contrived and too tightly packed.

Since the introduction of mixed ability English teaching in my school, I have become even more aware of the potential for imaginative writing which is within nearly all children. In her chapter 'The Basics and Remedial English' published in Bernard Harrison's *English Studies 11 – 18: an arts-based approach*, Bernadette Walsh says this:

> 'It is often held that a remedial secondary pupil must be taught "basic" technical skills ... before more sustained pieces of writing can be attempted. It is often held further, that if the pupils cannot read fluently in the first place, then what use is it in encouraging them to have an interest in literature or to enjoy poetry? If we wish the pupils really to possess and use the language, then we must give back to them access to their own experience. Only then may we help them discover their capacity for art-discourse.'

We deny children this discovery at a tremendous cost. It is no less than to exclude them from our common humanity. Their perceptions are no less fine, their feelings no less complex; their need to express personal experience is certainly no less acute. There is, however, a fine distinction between the kind of frustration which stimulates a positive and excited search for the right words in the right order, and the kind which dispirits and demoralises. There are those children whose grasp of language is so weak that withdrawal into small groups, or even teaching on an individual basis is essential if the wrong kind of frustration is not to develop into alienation. Nevertheless, even these children (two to three percent on average) are able to enjoy poetry and story and to develop the listening ear which is the basis of all language growth. As Bernadette Walsh says, this is to restore to them 'access to their own experience'. When this access is denied, there is no self-acceptance or self-respect. Indeed, a coming to terms with self through literature is a coming to terms with other people and environment.

Before the advent of mixed ability teaching in my school, I found myself at pains to choose 'suitable' poetry for the less able – poetry which was direct, made few linguistic demands and sometimes worked at a lower emotional level. Now, as I come to write this chapter, I find I have no programme for poetry marked 'for the less able'; they have been engaging at a much higher level and the poetry which I wished to anthologise in this book as representative of the less able has been written within the context of the strategies already outlined. The following poem, for example, was one of these children's attempts to create an 'Impossible Christmas Tree'. He easily understood the abstraction behind the idea. However, he had never heard of the word 'trim' used in this sense; 'Do you mean trim with a pair of scissors?' he asked as he prepared to write. Although he appeared to accept that to 'trim the tree' meant to 'decorate the tree', he clung on to his misunderstanding and turned it into metaphor in an unusual way.

Rainbow Tree

> First, I want a beaver to trim the tree
> To a sweet, comforting shape.
> Then, a rainbow to encircle the tree in its prism of light.
> At the top – a carp with its beautiful colours
> That reflect in the sun.
> Now I need a guard so man cannot harm it –
> A lion with a cloudlike mane
> And claws like icicles.
> Then my tree's beauty is complete
> For all to see.
>
> *Lee Clack, 12 years*

As an obsessive fisherman, he turned rightly to the roots of his experience, made connections, and wrote well at his own level.

I include this fable by the same child not because it is in any way good writing for a twelve year old but because again it demonstrates a child who has considerable technical difficulties and who does not read easily, nevertheless writing thoughtfully and with a sensitivity which is not lost in the ingenuousness and awkwardness of expression. Moreover, it is 'poetic' – he 'knows' his river in the poetic sense.

River

I walk round Holton Pit with the wind as strong as wood. I see a little boy
fishing with all the gear, shouting and splashing in the water. I wonder why
he came at all. Then there's an old man, so peaceful, watching his float go
up and down. Then, with no warning at all, it shoots along the pit like a
frightened rabbit. He plays the fish so gently so as not to hurt it. It comes to
the top. It's a carp. Then out comes the landing net. He picks it up with a
wet rag, then he slides it back so gently it is as if it were his own child. And
there are ducks playing in the reeds so nicely. Then the water shatters as
four birds land. And there's a wasp fighting so hard to save himself from
drowning. The man finishes. He throws the ducks bread. But all he throws
in are lead weights as heavy as death.

Lee Clack, 12 years

Similarly, the following poems were all written within the context of the work already
outlined in previous chapters. I feel they stand well beside the award-winning work
written by the average and above average. Above all, they are a justification of a
literature-based curriculum for *all* our children.

Bullfrog

In the river I sit,
on a leaf I stay,
watching the baby
floating down the river,
rocking gently on the shivery water
in the steamy sun.

I wonder why he is on the water.
I wonder why he is in the basket . . .
I wonder why . . .

But still I sit on the water,
on a leaf I stay,
still watching the baby drifting
dreamily away.

Marie Cantwell, 12 years

My Dog

My dog is a black bullet,
as sharp as a razor blade.
Its black fur feels soft
as if it had just been woven.
I feel that my dog comforts me.
When I take it for a walk I let if off
and it pants all this slather, a sort of polystyrene.
I call it back. It runs madly towards me.
It jumps on to my chest.
Its pink tongue feels as if it has been dry cleaned.
All the pink bumps on its tongue are sticky.
It feels as if it had just been dry cleaned
because it's so soft and rough.

Darren Mann, 11 years

Pigs

If you were to go in a pig shed
ten minutes before feeding time
the innocent-faced pigs
would squeal and jump up
and hang their legs over the side.
Then it would hurt
and they would flop back,
like old rags,
and walk around sniffing
the empty trough.
Then for the full ten minutes
until you had fed them
they would squeal and jump up
and flop back
down again.

If you were to walk in a pen
the squealing would stop
and you would hear quiet grunts
and you would feel a bottle-top nose
pushing at your legs
telling you to hurry up.

Then you could pour in the oats
all over their bottle-top noses.
But they wouldn't care;
they would go on eating
as if there was no more time left in the world.

Scott Baxter, 12 years

The Hanging Basket

The hanging basket
Hangs by a single link.
The firmly pressed peat
Holds the imprint of tiny fingers.
Dripping water has made a small puddle
And the reflection of a single red flower;
The splash of the hanging mushroom drip
Falls and dislodges the water,
The flower disappearing into a whirlpool.

Kevin Gowing, 12 years

13 Outlets

The act of writing does not end when the last word is written. The work must be presented. All written work requires this sense of audience (even a 'secret' diary). Somewhere there must be a receiver, somebody who notices what is said and responds. That response is part of the creative experience of the writer and is what we commonly call 'success'. It can happen at various levels and *must* happen if the writer's affirmation of identity within his text is to be confirmed. At the humblest level, this 'success' may be a line, a word, read aloud by the teacher to the child's accepting and appreciative contemporaries. It may be a piece of writing typed and displayed on the wall – the typed word gives a satisfying feeling of importance and recognition. Then, there is the school anthology which can disseminate poetry and story in to the local community. As we have already seen, there is the special dimension of the performing arts and, most importantly (because it reaches the widest audience and confirms the sense of identity most wholly), there is publication. It was Herbert Read's vision which first made children's writing accessible to the public at large when he founded what is known today as the W. H. Smith Young Writers' Competition. He believed that while children's writing was necessarily different from adults', it had a special quality of its own and should be read more widely. Today, the word 'competition' is suspect to some. I have found, however, that the excitement of disseminating writing to a wider public fuels the urge to write at all levels of ability. It is so much a matter of putting a high value on children's writing. Yes, some children's work will be selected for publication; others' will not. But the aspiration will be there for all. They will not be false aspirations, either, because all work in which there is genuine involvement and commitment will be valued and made public at one or more of the levels mentioned. Peter Abbs has said.

> 'we want art to penetrate as deeply as it can into both the individual and the community.'

If this is to happen children must engage with the community at both local and national level. We must not patronise them by withdrawing for fear of what we call success or failure. Within a healthy school environment there will be no sense of rejection but rather an underlining of the importance of both the group and the individual. At all costs, we must allow celebration of all art forms. I believe that the arts are in an increasingly beleaguered position in education today. They could be the bedrock of all achievement, including the scientific. In his foreword to *Young Words 1985* (the

collection of award winning entries in the W. H. Smith 'Young Writers' competition)
Andrew Davies writes:

> 'Teachers these days are belaboured with exhortations to get back to the
> basics (while going forward into the electronic age), with Philistine notions
> of relevance to a largely vanished world of mechanical labour, with reduc-
> tive programmes featuring 'Objectivity', 'Science and Technology' and
> 'Standards'. The illusory distinction between subjective and objective
> thinking was exploded long ago, principally by real scientists. The teachers
> of these fortunate children know that fostering creativity, lateral thinking,
> imaginative leaps is not only going to make poems and stories happen. It is
> keeping alive the kind of innovative thinking that produces breakthroughs
> in all intellectual fields.'

Certainly, poetry can be the most effective basis for our teaching of English. As the most
highly disciplined form of writing, it makes the greatest demands and is a sure path to
literacy. It is not enough to put children through certain grammatical hoops on the false
assumption that they will emerge literate and competent. This is a soft option which
simply does not work. Instead we must return to the richness of our culture and
immerse them in its literary forms (as we have seen, reading is an essentially active
pursuit when there is true engagement with the text) and then help them to find their
own voice within that culture. If successful, we will have a society of people in all walks
of life who write clearly and strongly, and who have assimilated correct grammatical
forms. They will, of course, also be a thinking people. We must never be traduced by
the soft option which neutralises thinking and enervates response.

References

Abbs, Peter (1982) *English Within the Arts* (Hodder and Stoughton)

Brownjohn, Sandy (1982) *What Rhymes With Secret?* (Hodder and Stoughton)

Church, Richard (1955) *Over the Bridge* (Heinemann)

Crossley-Holland, Kevin (1965) *The Battle of Maldon and Other Old English Poems* (MacMillan)

Davies, Andrew (1986) Foreword to *Young Words 1985* (MacMillan)

Fairfax, John; Moat, John (1981) *The Way to Write* (Elm Tree Books/Hamish Hamilton)

Garfield, Leon (1988) "A Grave Misunderstanding"; story in *Guardian Angels* ed. by Stephanie Netell (Puffin)

Garner, Alan (1965) *Elidor* (Collins)

Gordon, John (1975) "On Firm Ground"; essay in *The Thorny Paradise* ed. Edward Blishen (Kestrel Books)

Heaney, Seamus (1980) *Selected Poems 1965 – 75* (Faber)

Heinemann Educational Books (1976) *Children as Writers* 17th Daily Mirror Children's Literary Competition

Hopkins, Gerard Manley *The Journals and Papers of Gerard Manley Hopkins* Oxford University Press

Hines, Barry (1968) *A Kestrel for a Knave* (Penguin)

Hughes, Ted (1967) *Poetry in the Making* (Faber)

Hughes, Ted (1984) *What Is The Truth?* (Faber)

Lee, Laurie (1969) *Cider With Rosie* (The Hogarth Press)

Le Guin, Ursula (1973) *A Wizard of Earthsea* (Victor Gollancz)

Le Guin, Ursula (1975) "This Fear of Dragons"; essay in *The Thorny Paradise* ed. Edward Blishen (Kestrel Books)

Le Guin, Ursula (1973) Dreams Must Explain Themselves (Algol; reprinted in *Signal 19* 1976)

Nolan, Christopher (1987) *Under the Eye of the Clock* (Weidenfield and Nicholson)

Sanders, George (1971) *I Took My Mind a Walk* (Penguin English Stage One)

Stacey, Tom (1992); article in "Letters" ed. for RSL by David Hughes. "The Special Pact"

Tanner, Heather and Robin (1981) *Woodland Plants* (Robin Garton Ltd.)

Tomlinson, Charles (1985) *Eden: Graphics and Poetry* (Redcliffe Press Ltd.)

Turbina, Nika (1988) *First Draft* (Marion Boyars)

Walsh, Bernadette (1983) "The Basics and Remedial English"; chapter 4 in *English Studies 11 – 18; an arts-based approach* ed. Harrison, Bernard (Hodder and Stoughton

Acknowledgements

We are grateful for permission to reproduce the following material.

Pan Macmillian for the following: 'Bindweed' by Clair Honeywood, 'Dear Mummy' by Marilyn Rust, 'Whale' by Gavin Thurlow (all award winners of the 1993 W H Smith, Young Writers Competition to be published in 1994).

'The Dream of the Farmer' by Timothy Overtow, 'Blacksmith's Dream' by Deborah Swain, 'Gem' by Oliver Cooper, 'House of Reflections', 'Stick Insect' by Marilyn Rust (all award winners of the W H Smith, Young Writers Competition 1992. Published in *S is for Anaconda*, 1993). 'Hare' by William Muir, 'Time' by Joanne Ireland, 'Reflections' by Gemma White, 'Seal' by Jessica Brown, 'Gutting a Goose' by Tracy Martin, 'Astronaut' by Sara Worts, 'Fossil' by Jessica Brown, 'The Marshman' by Paul Batley, 'Snapdragon' by Emma Walkey (all from award winners of the W H Smith, Young Writers Competition 1991. Published in *Inky Foot, 1992*). 'The Maternity Ward' by Joanna Tuler, 'Robin' by Hannah Edwards, 'The Tadpole Is . . .' by Michelle Barnes, 'Grandad' by Edward Line, 'The Time of Day' by Stephen Garday, 'Mastitis' by Marnie Smith, 'The Winter Seashore' by Emma Buckingham, 'The Pheasant' by Hannah Edwards, 'Dunwich' by Stephen Gardam (all award winners of the W H Smith, Young Writers Competition 1990. Published in *Young Words 1991*). 'Memories' by Thomas Croft, 'Cat' by Stephen Gardam (all award winners of the W H Smith, Young Writers Competition 1989). Published in *Young Words 1990*. 'The Ford' by Clifford Black, 'The Truth of a Bullfinch' by Hilary Foster, 'Reflections' by Clifford Black, 'Reflection' by Thea Smiley, 'The Cow' by Kirsty Butcher, 'Nicholas' by Robert Aucock, 'The Journey' by Heidi Masters, 'Winter Churchyard' by Oliver Macdonald, (all from the award winners of the W H Smith, Young Writers Competition 1988. Published in *Young Words 1989*). 'The Grasshopper' by Helen Ward, 'Starling' by Helen Walkey, 'Flaming June' by Emma Graves, 'Winter' by Matthew Line, 'The Old Lady' by Robert Adcock, 'The Thought Cat' by Marie Fenn, 'Chickey Lucky' by Caroline English (all from award winners of the W H Smith, Young Writers Competition 1987. Published in *Young Words 1988*). 'Senses' by Ruth Kingshott (award winner in the W H Smith, Young Writers Competition 1986. Published in *Young Words 1987*).

Our thanks also to the following: Marion Boyars Publishers Ltd. for 'Stop for an Instant' by Nika Turbina; Oxford University Press for 'To Be Engraved on the Skull of a Cormorant' and 'Winter Piece', both from Charles Tomlinson's *Collected Poems* (OUP 1985) and the use of the extract from *The Journals and Papers of Gerard Manley Hopkins* edited by Humphry House and Graham Storey, (OUP 1959); David Higham Associates for 'My Grandmother' by Elizabeth Jennings from *Collected Poems 1986*; Penguin Books for 'The Door' by Miroslau Holub from *Modern European Poets* translated by Ian Milner and George Theiner 1967; The National Exhibition of Children's

About WWF

WWF is an international environmental organisation with national groups around the world. Launched in 1961, WWF has supported over 5,000 projects in 130 countries, and has invested over £230 million in conservation over the last 10 years.

WWF UK is committed to a broadly based environmental education programme. As part of this programme, resource materials are produced which aim to enable teachers to bring environmental issues into everyday classroom teaching, and to give young people the knowledge and experience they need in order to make informed personal judgements about these issues.

Resources are being developed for subjects across the entire school curriculum, making use of the inherent qualities of each subject in order to develop specific aspects of environmental understanding and sensitivity. In addition, WWF has in progress projects designed to help teachers plan, implement and evaluate effective cross-curricular environmental education.

'Reaching Out', WWF's INSET programme for Primary and Secondary teachers, is now available on a regional basis across the UK. Also in development are a number of innovative electronic data delivery projects which will give schools, colleges and individuals access to WWF's expertise, data, reports and fact sheets.

In addition to courses and resources, WWF runs a free Teacher Representative Scheme for all schools. Registered schools receive WWF's termly teachers' newsletter, Lifelines, details of all new resources, plus a discount on all education materials.

If you would like further details about WWF's education programme, please write to:

WWF UK, Education, Panda House, Weyside Park, Godalming, Surrey GU7 1XR, or telephone: 0483 426444.